职业教育高速铁路客运服务专业系列教材

HIGH-SPEED RAILWAY PASSENGER SERVICE ENGLISH

高速铁路客运服务英语

王 蕊　王 丹　主　编
杨 丽　孙雯雯　副主编
王德恩　宋秀秋　主　审

人民交通出版社股份有限公司
北　京

内 容 提 要

《高速铁路客运服务英语》为职业教育高速铁路客运服务专业系列教材之一。全书共分为4个模块，模块Ⅰ为高速铁路概述，主要内容包括高速铁路简介、高速铁路历史与文化、高速铁路旅行指南、高速铁路"八纵八横"客运专线以及"一带一路"背景下的高速铁路；模块Ⅱ侧重于车站服务工作，主要内容包括售票服务、进站服务、候车服务、检票服务、站台服务、出站服务等；模块Ⅲ侧重于列车服务工作，主要内容包括迎乘服务、车厢服务、餐饮服务；模块Ⅳ包括特殊旅客服务、应急情况与服务等内容。

本教材适于作为高职高专高速铁路客运服务专业、铁道交通运营管理专业、城市轨道交通运营管理专业等大学一、二年级学生的教学用书，还可作为国家铁路、地方铁路、城市轨道交通相关企业人员的培训教材。

图书在版编目（CIP）数据

高速铁路客运服务英语/王蕊，王丹主编.—北京：
人民交通出版社股份有限公司，2021.11
ISBN 978-7-114-17397-4

Ⅰ.①高… Ⅱ.①王…②王… Ⅲ.①高速铁路—铁路运输—客运服务—英语 Ⅳ.①U293.3

中国版本图书馆CIP数据核字（2021）第110312号

职业教育高速铁路客运服务专业系列教材
Gaosu Tielu Keyun Fuwu Yingyu

书　　名：	**高速铁路客运服务英语**
著 作 者：	王　蕊　王　丹
责任编辑：	李　晴
责任校对：	孙国靖　宋佳时
责任印制：	张　凯
出版发行：	人民交通出版社股份有限公司
地　　址：	(100011)北京市朝阳区安定门外外馆斜街3号
网　　址：	http://www.ccpcl.com.cn
销售电话：	(010)59757973
总 经 销：	人民交通出版社股份有限公司发行部
经　　销：	各地新华书店
印　　刷：	中国电影出版社印刷厂
开　　本：	787×1092　1/16
印　　张：	10.75
字　　数：	261千
版　　次：	2021年11月　第1版
印　　次：	2023年8月　第2次印刷
书　　号：	ISBN 978-7-114-17397-4
定　　价：	45.00元

（有印刷、装订质量问题的图书由本公司负责调换）

活页式装订说明

为更好地贯彻执行《国家职业教育改革实施方案》（国发〔2019〕4号）中"倡导使用新型活页式、工作手册式教材"的理念，本教材在以模块化、任务化方式组织教学内容的基础上，在全书印刷了活页孔位置，师生可根据实际教学需求，将教材拆分打孔后放入B5纸张9孔型标准活页夹，装订成活页式教材后使用。

装订成活页式教材可实现"教材""学材"的融合和提升，具体如下：

1. "教材"的内容组合与动态更新

（1）可凸显教材的模块化、任务化特征，方便教学设计，教师可根据实际需求调整教学顺序。

（2）可根据不同教学要求，替换、删减、添加教学内容和教辅资料，如调整或补充典型案例、行业热点、地方特色的相关素材，以及"岗课赛证"融通的相关内容等。

2. "学材"的优化整理与灵活使用

（1）可将学习笔记、参考资料等添加至教材相应位置，辅助学习。

（2）可根据教学要求随堂携带对应页码部分，轻松方便。

（3）可根据个人认知情况和其他实际需求，调整内容顺序，巩固学习效果。

前言 PREFACE

【编写背景】

为适应我国高等职业教育的发展，为铁路交通事业培养优秀人才，推动教学改革的不断深入，贯彻落实《国家职业教育改革实施方案》（国发〔2019〕4号）文件精神，我们深入了解了铁路企业用人需求以及客运涉外服务工作要求，组织相关职业院校具有丰富经验的专业教师及铁路行业专家精心编写了本教材。

【课程定位】

教材的编写结合铁路客运专业教学内容，结合一线工作实践，遵照铁路客运工作的相关工作过程，力求提升高职英语教材的适用性、职业性和实践性。本教材可作为高等职业教育高速铁路客运服务专业、城市轨道交通运营管理专业的基础课程教材，还可作为铁路、城市轨道运输相关企业人员的培训教材，可供行业相关人员在实际工作中参考阅读。

【特色创新】

1. 匹配职业技能。教材对接最新职业标准、行业标准和岗位规范，紧贴高速铁路工作岗位实际工作过程，按照高速铁路概述、车站服务、列车服务、应急服务四大模块对客运英语知识进行全方位阐述。每个模块都包含教学目标、广播播报、工作对话、语音知识以及有关铁路行业新情况、新规定和新发展的英文阅读，学生通过知识学习和技能练习，能够全面提高高铁客运服务工作过程中的英语听、说、读、写、译能力。

2. 突出思政教学。 教材内容四大模块突出内容与思政相结合。高速铁路概述模块内容与我国铁路发展历史相结合，增强学生的爱国热情与自豪感；车站服务、列车服务模块内容融入责任意识、忠于职守等德育内容，提升学生的职业道德意识；应急服务模块内容与公共卫生安全结合，使学生增强制度自信，加深对人类命运共同体理念的理解。

3. 注重交际训练。 教材中每个单元都设置了工作对话及语音知识的训练指导和练习重点，以帮助学生树立信心，练习英语口语发音，使学生英语口语流利、顺畅，从而培养学生用英语进行客运服务交际的实用能力。

【编写分工】

本教材由高等院校优秀英语教师、铁路专业教师和铁路行业专家合作编写，由黑龙江交通职业技术学院王蕊、湖南铁路科技职业技术学院王丹担任主编，黑龙江交通职业技术学院杨丽、孙雯雯担任副主编。本教材编写人员具体分工为：模块Ⅰ中1、2单元，模块Ⅱ中4、8单元，模块Ⅲ中11单元及模块Ⅳ由王蕊编写；模块Ⅱ中3、5单元由杨丽编写；模块Ⅱ中6、7单元由王丹编写；模块Ⅲ中9、10单元由孙雯雯编写。王蕊负责编写教材提纲和全书的统稿工作。全书由中国铁路哈尔滨局集团有限公司哈尔滨客运段王德恩、中国铁路哈尔滨局集团有限公司哈尔滨职工培训基地宋秀秋主审。

【致谢】

本教材的编写得到了黑龙江交通职业技术学院刘英哲和倪磊的大力支持，同时借鉴了铁道交通运营管理专业相关网络资源，在此表示衷心的感谢。虽然编写团队在教材编写过程中进行了精心的内容设计和凝练，但书中难免存在不足和疏漏之处，敬请广大读者和同行批评指正。

作　者

2021年6月

目录 CONTENTS

Section I	Overview of High-speed Railway	1
Unit 1	Introduction of High-speed Railway	2
Unit 2	High-speed Railway Travel Guide	12
Section II	Station Service	23
Unit 3	Ticket Service	24
Unit 4	Security Check	34
Unit 5	Waiting Service	43
Unit 6	Ticket Checking	53
Unit 7	Platform Service	63
Unit 8	Arrival	74
Section III	Train Service	83
Unit 9	Boarding Service	84
Unit 10	Carriage Service	93
Unit 11	Dining Service	103
Section IV	Special and Emergency Service	113
Unit 12	Special and Emergency Service	114
Appendix		125
Appendix I	High-speed Railway Broadcast	126
Appendix II	Basic Knowledge of Phonetics	134
Appendix III	Railway Service Rules	140
Appendix IV	Terms of High-speed Railway both in Chinese and in English	148
Appendix V	Abbreviations for High-speed Railway	151
Appendix VI	Service Expressions	152
References		164

Section I
Overview of High-speed Railway

Unit 1 Introduction of High-speed Railway

Goals

Know history about High-speed Railway;
Learn how to introduce the cultures of China's High-speed Railway;
Learn how to get to the railway station;
Grasp the expressions of regional culture in the design of High-speed Railway stations.

Warming-up

Try to think

Task 1 Match the full names with the logos.

Train à Grande Vitesse	Alta Velocidad Española
European Star	Japan Railways
China's High-speed Railway	Inter City Express
Korea Train Express	Acceleration and Excellence Express

1._____ 2._____ 3._____ 4._____

5. _____   6. _____   7. _____   8. _____

Task 2 What is the meaning of CRH design?

Try to listen

The High-speed Railway broadcasting

Task 1 Listen carefully and fill in the blanks with what you hear.

Attention please! We are doing thermal _____ to each passenger for the interest of _____ health. Thank you for your cooperation! Once it is done, you can enter the _____ room. There is an internet _____ and a reading room inside, where you can surf the internet, and find some Chinese and English books and _____.

Task 2 Read the paragraph in Task 1 loudly and try to recite it.

Task 1 Retell the conversations below and imitate the pronunciation and intonation after listening to the recordings.

   C 1 Regional cultural elements in the railway station (车站与地域文化)

   P=Passenger   S=Station staff

P: Hi, I just came back from Qufu.

S: That is great. How do you like Qufudong Railway Station?

P: It's fantastic. The station incorporates many local cultural elements.

S: That is not surprising. The design of High-speed Railway Station is based on the culture of a city.

P: Confucian culture integrates into its design.

S: China is a country with a long history. Traditional and regional culture is reflected in the railway stations everywhere. I hope you will enjoy the great Chinese culture during your stay.

P: Thank you very much.

Word Tips

fantastic	[fæn'tæstɪk]	adj.	极好的	regional	['riːdʒənl]	adj.	地区的
incorporate	[ɪn'kɔːpəreɪt]	v.	包含	reflect	[rɪ'flekt]	v.	反映
integrate	['ɪntɪɡreɪt]	v.	(使)融入	Confucian culture			儒家文化

C 2   About different types of high-speed trains (高速列车种类)

David: Dear Ms. Smith, would you please tell me how many types of high-speed trains are there in China?

Ms. Smith: Sure. There are three types: G-trains, D-trains, and C-trains.

David: Which one is the fastest?

Ms. Smith: The G-trains is the fastest.

David: How fast the G-trains can go?

Ms. Smith: They are said to go up to 605 km/h.

David: Which country's High-speed Railway mileage tops the world?

Ms. Smith: China, of course.

David: I will study hard and work for China's High-speed Railway in the future.

Ms. Smith: Sounds great!

Task 2   Read and role-play the conversations in pairs.

C 1

A= Passenger A   B= Passenger B

A: What is the oldest train currently preserved in China?

B: It is the Class Zero Steam Locomotives.

A: Was it made in China?

B: No, it was made in England in 1881. It can only go 20 km/h.

A: That's really slow!

B: This is a Dong Feng diesel locomotive made in China in 1966.

A: How fast will it go?

B: It can go up to 100 km/h, which is a lot faster than a steam locomotive.

A: Look! This is Shaoshan-type electric locomotive.

B: It is one of its first kind in China and can go up to 90 km/h.

A: Do you want to have a look inside?

B: Sure. The control panel looks like piano keys.

A: There was once a very popular song in China, and a part of its lyrics is: with the spinning of the wheels and the sound of the siren, the train runs quickly towards Shaoshan. Have you heard about it?

B: No, I can search it online though.

A: Hooray! "China Star!"

B: Yes. It was made in 2002 and can go over 300 km/h.

A: How amazing!

C 2

B: This is the Zhangjiajiexi Railway Station. Welcome to Zhangjiajie.

A: Thank you. What a beautiful station!

B: The overall appearance is undulating. The waiting room resembles to Tujia stilted building.

A: It's amazing. How many pairs of trains are operating along the Qianjiang-Changde railway route?

B: There are more than 27 pairs: 12 pairs of EMU daily lines, 8 pairs of peak lines and 7 pairs of ordinary speed trains etc.

A: It is so convenient! What's the meaning of EMU?

B: EMU means Electric Multiple Units.

A: Got it. Thank you.

C 3

A: Excuse me, I am looking for the railway station. The mobile navigation shows that it is right here but I can't find it.

B: The railway station? You need to go down this street and turn left at the first corner to the Railway Street. The station is at the end of the street.

A: How long will it take to get there?

B: It only takes about five minutes.

A: Okay, got it. I think I will be able to find it. Thank you.

B: Not at all.

Task 3 Situational practice

Situation 1: Suppose you are a staff member at the information desk. A passenger wants to know how his/her friend gets to Shanghai Railway Station from Huangpu District, Yu Garden. Make a conversation with your partner and try to practice it. You can refer to the following information.

By subway: Walk to People's Square (人民广场) Subway Station. Take Metro Line 1 (toward the Fujin Road Station). Get off the train at Shanghai Railway Station Subway Station. The trip takes about 30 minutes in total.

By taxi: It takes about 14 minutes and 20 yuan.

Situation 2: Suppose you are a staff member at the information desk. A passenger wants to know the characteristics of Wuhan Railway Station. What would you tell him/her? Make a conversation with your partner and try to practice it. You can refer to the Culture of High-speed Railway Stations in China of Knowledge Stock.

Task 4 Additional practice: phonetics (Front vowels)

1. Pronunciation methods

[i:]

发[i:]音的常见字母与字母组合有e、ee、ea、ie、i、y。[i:]是长元音，要把音发足。

发音方法：舌尖抵下齿，舌前部尽量向上抬高，口形扁平(与微笑时的口形相似)。

[i]

发[i]音的常见字母与字母组合有i、e、u、y、ey、ay。

发音方法：舌尖抵下齿，舌前部抬高，舌位比[i:]略低，口形扁平。

[e]

发[e]音的常见字母与字母组合有a、e、ea、ai。

发音方法：舌尖抵下齿，舌前部稍抬起，舌位比[i:]低；唇形中长，开口度比[i:]大。

[æ]

字母a在重读闭音节中发[æ]音。

发音方法：舌尖抵下齿，舌前部稍抬高，舌位比[e]更低；双唇平伸，呈扁平形。

2. Read and practice

[i:]	speed	we	leaf	sheet	piece	read
[i]	minute	his	begin	sunny	money	village
[e]	said	many	shell	pleasure	anywhere	desk
[æ]	map	happy	bad	flag	transfer	ash

High-speed Railway

High-speed Railway (HSR) is a type of rail transport that runs faster than traditional rail traffic. Multiple definitions for High-speed Railway are in use worldwide. Though there is no single standard in the world, new lines in excess of 250 km/h and existing lines in excess of 200 km/h are widely considered to be high-speed.

The first High-speed Railway system, the Shinkansen, known as the bullet train, began to operate in Japan in 1964, in time for the first Tokyo Olympics. Many countries have built and developed High-speed Railway infrastructures to connect major cities, including France, Germany, Turkey, the United States and so on. Only in Europe did High-speed Railway cross international borders at first. China has built over 35000 kilometers of High-speed Railway at the end of 2019 and plans to increase its High-speed Railway network year by year. China has built the world's biggest HSR network.

The list of High-speed Railway history and development worldwide is shown below:

1964-1990	Japan: the birth of High-speed Railway
	Germany: the birth of The TGV (Train à Grande Vitesse)
1990-Mid 1990s	Europe: an international High-speed Railway network
Mid 1990s-now	HSR services spreading in the world
	China: surpassing the rest of the world

Words and Expressions

rail	[reɪl]	n.	铁路；铁轨	infrastructure	[ˈɪnfrəstrʌktʃə]	n.	基础建设
transport	[ˈtrænspɔːt]	n.	交通运输系统	network	[ˈnetwɜːk]	n.	网状系统
multiple	[ˈmʌltɪpl]	adj.	多种多样的	spread	[spred]	v.	扩展
definition	[ˌdefɪˈnɪʃn]	n.	定义	surpass	[səˈpɑːs]	v.	超过
standard	[ˈstændəd]	n.	标准	Tokyo	[ˈtəʊkiəʊ]	n.	东京
excess	[ɪkˈses]	n.	超过	Shinkansen			日本新干线
bullet	[ˈbʊlɪt]	n.	子弹	Turkey			土耳其

Task 1 Choose the best answer.

1. The operating speed reaching _____ is widely considered to be high-speed train.
   A. more than 300 km/h   B. less than 200 km/h   C. more than 200 km/h
2. Which country built the first High-speed Railway?
   A. America.   B. German.   C. Japan.
3. Does China's High-speed Railway mileage top the world?
   A. Not mentioned.   B. Yes, it does.   C. No, it doesn't.
4. How many stages are there in the development of High-speed Railway?
   A. Four stages.   B. Three stages.   C. Five stages.
5. An international high-speed network was first built in _____.
   A. Europe   B. Asia   C. North America

Task 2 Translate the following sentences into Chinese.

1. High-speed Railway (HSR) is a type of rail transport that runs faster than traditional rail traffic.

2. New lines in excess of 250 km/h and existing lines in excess of 200 km/h are widely considered to be high-speed.
_____

3. The first High-speed Railway system, the Shinkansen, known as the bullet train, began to operate in Japan in 1964, in time for the first Tokyo Olympics.
_____

4. China has built over 35000 kilometers of High-speed Railway at the end of 2019 and plans to increase its High-speed Railway network year by year.
_____

5. China has built the world's biggest HSR network.
_____

Task 3　Fill in the blanks according to the Chinese meanings.

Introduction of a Train Station

_____(杭州东火车站) was officially put into use on 1 July 2013. It is one of the largest _____(交通枢纽) in China, even in Asia. The station brings together high-speed rails, ordinary trains, _____(专列), metro, maglev, public transportation, waterways and other modes of transportation and ancillary services in one.

Name: 杭州东火车站
Address: _____(浙江省杭州市江干区天城路185号)
Station Size: 15 platforms and 30 lines for ordinary or high-speed trains; 3 platforms and 4 lines for maglev
Subway: _____(地铁4号线)

Task 1　Complete the flow chart after discussing in groups what service the passengers receive in order.

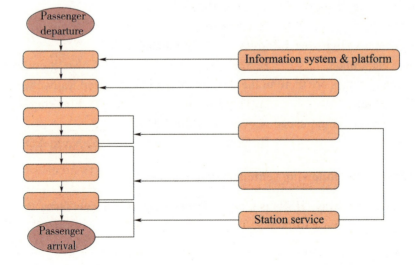

Task 2 Match the English in column A with their corresponding Chinese in column B.

A	B
Waiting for a train	途中运行
Buying tickets	下车
Train service	列车服务
Running on route	购票
Buying tickets	上车
Station service	车站服务
Information inquiry	信息查询
Getting off a train	候车
Boarding a train	售票

1. Architecture elements of some High-speed Railway stations in China

Theme	Railway station	Introduction
Charm of ancient capital	Beijingnan Railway Station	The station's roof was inspired by the upturned hip roofs of the Temple of Heaven nearby. The design integrates the traditional cultural elements of the classical building "triple eaves"
Marine culture	Binhai Railway Station (Yujiapu High-speed Railway Station)	The shell-shaped dome was built with a steel and membrane-integrated structure, which allows passengers to see views 360 degrees around. The station is also the first monolayer long-span steel structure with a latticed dome in the world. It is also the world's largest and deepest underground station

Theme	Railway station	Introduction
Nine-headed bird	Wuhan Railway Station	The design was inspired by the yellow crane, the symbol of Wuhan City. The distinctive roof is intended to resemble the crane's wings, and is based on a sine curve. The building consists of nine separated parts, symbolizing China's nine provinces, plus a central thoroughfare
Ancient bridge culture	Shijiazhuang Railway Station	It is a modern large traffic hub center of the "Four Vertical and Four Horizontal" High-speed Railway network. Arch bridge is the subject of the station, and the project is a building-bridge combined structure
Leaves of bananas in flower city	Guangzhounan Railway Station	It is a design of the combination of elevated bridge with building structure. Its design has distinct Lingnan cultural characteristics. Its huge glass dome is like banana leaves

2. "Eight Vertical and Eight Horizontal" railway network in China

- **Eight Verticals** (north-south direction)

(1) Coastal Passageway

(2) Beijing-Shanghai Passageway

(3) Beijing-Hong Kong (Taipei) Passageway

(4) Harbin-Hong Kong (Macau) Passageway

(5) Hohhot-Nanning Passageway

(6) Beijing-Kunming Passageway

(7) Baotou (Yinchuan)-Hainan Passageway

(8) Lanzhou (Xining)-Guangzhou Passageway

- **Eight Horizontals** (east-west direction)

(1) Suifenhe-Manzhouli Passageway

(2) Beijing-Lanzhou Passageway
(3) Qingdao-Yinchuan Passageway
(4) Eurasia Continental Bridge Passageway
(5) Yangtze River Passageway
(6) Shanghai-Kunming Passageway
(7) Xiamen-Chongqing Passageway
(8) Guangzhou-Kunming Passageway

3. High-speed Railway serves for the belt and road initiative

The construction of High-speed Railways in China began with the building of the Qinhuangdao-Shenyang High-speed Railway in 1999.

China's first self-built High-speed Railway, the Beijing-Tianjin Intercity Railway with a maximum speed of 350 km/h, opened in 2018, marking the beginning of China's High-speed Railway era.

The Beijing-Tianjin Intercity Railway has become a national icon that showcases the country's development achievements and the quality of its High-speed Railways.

Chinese government had spent $300 million building the largest and fastest HSR system in the world by 2020. It's said that the trains can run 400 km/h and create new business for China and other countries through the Belt and Road.

In addition, China's High-speed Railway construction companies have been expanding overseas, benefiting other countries with their cutting-edge technology, high quality, and superior services.

China has built the Ankara-Istanbul High-speed Railway in Turkey, the Jakarta-Bandung High-speed Railway in India, and the Moscow-Kazan High-speed Railway in Russia and Tatarstan.

4. China's High-speed Railway development situation

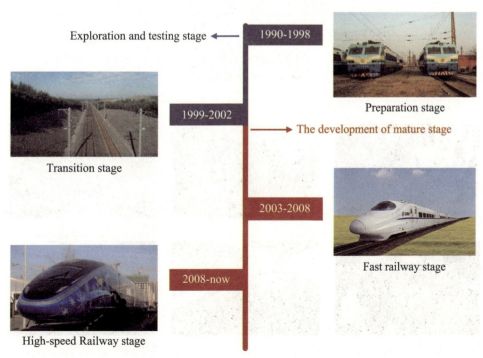

Unit 2 High-speed Railway Travel Guide

Goals

Learn about boarding procedures;
Learn about the High-speed Railway travel safety tips;
Learn to use Alipay correctly in China for foreigners when taking high-speed trains;
Learn how to get to the railway station.

Warming-up

Try to think

Task 1   Match the words and expressions with the pictures.

Get on board	Security	Settle luggage
Ticket checking	Exit upon arrival	Purchase tickets
Enjoy trip	Wait for boarding	Go to platform

1._____

2._____

3._____

4._____

5._____

6._____

7._____ 8._____ 9._____

Task 2 Do you choose high-speed train to travel for business or leisure? If so, Why?

Try to listen

The High-speed Railway broadcasting

Task 1 Listen carefully and fill in the blanks with what you hear.

For a smooth trip, please carry valid travel document with validated endorsement. Passengers _____ to go through the mainland exit or Hong Kong _____ procedures should take the _____ train back to the mainland with the assistance of station staff and pay ticket _____ and service _____ for the trip.

Task 2 Read the paragraph in Task 1 loudly and try to recite it.

Task 1 Retell the conversations below and imitate the pronunciation and intonation after listening to the recordings.

C 1 About West Kowloon Station (西九龙车站简介)

David　　　: Good afternoon.
Zhang Wei: Good afternoon, sir.
David　　　: Could you tell me if Macau has High-speed Railway?
Zhang Wei: No, Macau has no Railway service.
David　　　: How about Hong Kong?
Zhang Wei: Hong Kong has a High-speed Railway service. The station is West Kowloon.
David　　　: When did it start operating?
Zhang Wei: It was put into service in 2018. It is the fastest way for inter-city traveling.
David　　　: How many cities do it serve?
Zhang Wei: It serves 58 major mainland cities with no interchanges now.
David　　　: What about its service?
Zhang Wei: There is a range of station and shopping facilities at the station plus different classes of travel and on-board facilities offer you a hassle-free journey.

David   : That is great. Thank you.
Zhang Wei: You are welcome.

Word Tips

Macau	[məˈkaʊ]	n.	澳门	hassle-free			快捷
West Kowloon			西九龙				

C 2 "Four New Great Inventions" (新四大发明)

Liu Tao: Do you know what is the "Four Great Inventions" of ancient China?
Tom   : Of course, they are papermaking, gunpowder, printing and the compass.
Liu Tao: We now have a new phrase called the "four new great inventions" in China.
Tom   : Interesting. What are they?
Liu Tao: They are High-speed Railway, mobile payment, e-commerce, and bike-sharing.
Tom   : Who came up with the term of "four new inventions"?
Liu Tao: The term has been repeatedly quoted in Chinese state media since 2017.
Tom   : How the four inventions were selected?
Liu Tao: It first appeared in a survey result conducted by Beijing Foreign Studies University in May 2017. It asked people from 20 countries about what technology they "most wanted to bring back" to their countries from China. The fours are the most wanted.
Tom   : I see. This is the respondents' top answers.
Liu Tao: China has been putting strong effort on technological innovation as she seeks to become an "innovation nation" by 2020.
Tom   : Ok. I see. High-speed Railway tops the rank.
Liu Tao: That is correct.

Word Tips

gunpowder	[ˈgʌnpaʊdə]	n.	火药	quote	[kwəʊt]	v.	引用
compass	[ˈkʌmpəs]	n.	指南针	media	[ˈmiːdiə]	n.	媒体
term	[tɜːm]	n.	词语	survey	[ˈsɜːveɪ]	n.	民意调查
conduct	[kənˈdʌkt]	v.	组织	top	[tɒp]	adj.	最高级别的

technology	[tek'nɒlədʒi]	n.	科技	rank	[ræŋk]	n.	地位
respondent	[rɪ'spɒndənt]	n.	回答问题的人	mobile payment			移动支付
effort	['efət]	n.	努力	e-commerce			电商；网购
innovation	[ˌɪnə'veɪʃn]	n.	创新；改革	bike-sharing			共享单车
seek	[si:k]	v.	争取；谋求	come up			提出

Task 2　Read and role-play the conversations in pairs.

C 1

A=Passenger A　B=Passenger B

A: I've decided to escape the Beijing Winter chilly.

B: Where are you going?

A: I'll travel hundreds of kilometers to the south of China to tropical Yunnan and go to feed pigeons.

B: It is a long trip and will take about 10 hours and 49 minutes.

A: You think so! I think I'll be there before dinner!

B: I am going to Tianjin.

A: That is good. Are you going anywhere else after that?

B: Not really. It is a business trip. After it is done, I am going straight back to Beijing.

A: It is a short trip.

B: I have a lot of work waiting for me.

A: You will be fine. Good luck!

C 2

A: What is your nationality?

B: I am from Holland.

A: Welcome to China. Holland is a very beautiful county. Where have you been in China?

B: I have been in Beijing for 2 months and visited Tianjin once during weekend. I plan to tour around before going back to Holland.

A: That is a good idea. Did you take high-speed train before?

B: Yes, when I travelled to Tianjin.

A: What do you think about the High-speed Railway?

B: I think it is awesome. It is very convenient and fast.

A: That is true. I like it, too. It is my top choice for short to medium distance traveling. Does Holland have High-speed Railway service?

B: Not as comparable as here. It is not that fast.

A: What is the average speed of trains in Holland?

B: It is from 120 to 140 km/h.

A: I heard that China plans to make even faster trains and the highest speed can reach up to 1000 km/h.

B: 1000 km/h? That is fast!

A: Yes. That is what I heard.

B: Wow, if this is true, it will take only one hour to Beijing.

A: Exactly. It will make traveling even more convenient.

B: That is exciting!

C 3

A: Ladies and gentlemen, the next station is Chengdu Railway Station. Passengers to Chengdu please get your luggage ready to get off the train.

B: How long will it take to arrive at the station?

A: About 20 minutes.

B: Thank you. I heard that it is a very beautiful city.

A: Yes, you are right.

B: I heard that a king of the ancient Shu Kingdom established its capital in the center of Sichuan plain and named it Chengdu thousands of years ago.

A: You are right. Now Chengdu is one of the top tourism cities in China. And there are many places of interest.

B: It sounds great! Are there any attractions worth visiting?

A: You can go to see Jiuzhaigou National Park, it is a nature reserve in the north of Sichuan.

B: Wonderful! Could you tell me more about it?

A: Jiuzhaigou, literally meaning "the nine stockaded-village valley", is named after the Tibetan-style villages situated in the valley.

B: What is that?

A: The clear and colorful waters, the green and golden trees and the lofty snow mountains constitute the unique beauty.

B: Really? It sounds like a paradise. Anything else?

A: E'mei Mountain and Leshan Giant Buddha are both worth visiting. Of course, food in Chengdu is very delicious, especially the snack and hotpot. You must have a try.

B: It sounds very attractive. Thank you very much.

A: My pleasure, and if you have any questions, please tell me at any time.

Task 3 Situational practice

Situation 1: Suppose you are a staff member in the Railway station. A passenger will go to Hong Kong from Shenzhen. You offer help to him/her for meeting his/her requirements. Make a conversation with your partner and try to practice it. The following is for your reference.

- Short distance between Hong Kong and Shenzhen.
- Trains to/from Shenzhen (Shenzhenbei and Futian stations).
- Travel time is 16 to 20 minutes with departures from 6:44 to 22:50.
- Shenzhen has two stations for high-speed trains: Shenzhen north station and Futian station. It has 80 pairs of trains per day.
- Price:
  Business class：¥226.
  1st class：¥120.
  2nd class：¥75.

Situation 2: Suppose you are a staff member in the Railway station. A passenger is going to Xi'an for tourism. What scenic spots would you recommend and how would you introduce these scenic spots in Xi'an to the passenger? Make a conversation with your partner and try to practice it. The following is for your reference.

- The scenic spots: Dayan Pagoda, Xi'an Bell and Drum Tower, The Terra Cotta Warriors.
- be located in…
- a landmark building of Xi'an.
- China's largest ancient military museum.

Task 4　Additional practice: phonetics (Central vowels)

1. Pronunciation methods

[ə:]

发[ə:]音的常见字母与字母组合有er、ir、ur、or、ear。

发音方法：舌身平放，舌中部稍抬，舌尖抵下齿底部；双唇呈扁平口形，自然张开。

[ə]

发[ə]音的常见字母与字母组合有a、or、er、ar、ure、e。

发音方法：舌身平放，舌尖轻抵下齿底部，舌中部略隆起，比发[ɜ:]时低些。双唇呈扁平口形，比发[ə:]时略张开些。

[ʌ]

发[ʌ]音的常见字母与字母组合有u、o、oo、ou。

发音方法：舌尖和舌端两侧轻触下齿，舌后部靠前部分稍抬起，嘴唇微微张开，伸向两边，唇形稍扁。

2. Read and practice

[ə:]	fur	serve	dirty	curtain	early	world
[ə]	petite	picture	dinner	sugar	doctor	panda
[ʌ]	trust	money	luck	brush	touch	country

Tips for Safe Travel

Many people now choose to travel by high-speed train and find it comfortable and safe, normally without any delay.

So here are some safety tips for travelers taking trains.

When waiting for a train:

Keep your belongings in front of you as the train stations are always crowded.

When boarding a train:

If you are traveling with children, keep an eye on them especially in large crowds. There may be pushing and shoving!

Wait for the train at the assigned platform and the safe region.

When on a train:

Passengers should announce arrivals timely if catching the wrong train or missing the destination station.

Make sure luggage is securely within the edge of the rack above the seats to avoid accidents. Try to place luggage in sight in case someone takes it by mistake.

Take good care of your children. In order to avoid any unexpected accident, do not let them run in the carriage, climb the seats, hold the crack of the door, or touch the electric water boiler.

Self-service hot water is available in the carriage. For safety reason, read the instruction before using the water dispensers. When adjusting the back of the chair, be careful of the service table behind you because there may be hot water on it.

Smoking is not allowed anywhere in the train including toilet and passenger way. In case someone smokes, smoke alarms will ring automatically, and the train will slow down and delay the schedule.

Safety devices are marked in red only be used in an emergency. Do not touch them to avoid accident.

Have your belongings in advance for your destination. Do not forget your belongings or take other luggage by mistake when getting off. The train will only stop for a short time, so do not get off the train if it isn't your destination.

For your own safety, do not gather round or lean against the train door.

Don't get off the train before it fully stops. Be aware of the gap between the train and the platform. In case of snow or rain, the platform may be slippery. Please mind your steps.

Words and Expressions

tip	[tɪp]	n.	实用的提示	instruction	[ɪn'strʌkʃn]	n.	说明;指南
normally	['nɔːməli]	adv.	通常	dispenser	[dɪ'spensə(r)]	n.	自动取物装置
delay	[dɪ'leɪ]	n.	延迟	adjust	[ə'dʒʌst]	v.	调整
belongings	[bɪ'lɒŋɪŋz]	n.	随身物品	alarm	[ə'lɑːm]	n.	警报
crowded	['kraʊdɪd]	adj.	拥挤的	automatically	[ˌɔːtə'mætɪkli]	adv.	自动地
shove	[ʃʌv]	v.	推挤	emergency	[i'mɜːdʒənsi]	n.	突发事件
assign	[ə'saɪn]	v.	指定	avoid	[ə'vɔɪd]	v.	避免

platform	['plætfɔ:m]	n.	站台	lean	[li:n]	v.	倚靠
region	['ri:dʒən]	n.	地区	aware	[ə'weə(r)]	adj.	知道的
announce	[ə'naʊns]	v.	通知	gap	[gæp]	n.	间隙
destination	[ˌdestɪ'neɪʃn]	n.	目的地	slippery	['slɪpəri]	adj.	滑的
edge	[edʒ]	n.	边;边缘	by accident			意外地
crack	[kræk]	n.	缝隙	slow down			(使)放慢
electric	[ɪ'lektrɪk]	adj.	电的	by mistake			错误地
available	[ə'veɪləbl]	adj.	可获得的	in advance			提前

Task 1　Read the text and decide whether the following statements are T (true) or F (false).

(　) 1. Passengers can wait for a train at any place on the platform.

(　) 2. Children can't run in the carriage.

(　) 3. Smoking is allowed on trains.

(　) 4. Passengers can touch the devices with red marks so as to avoid any accident.

(　) 5. Passengers should get off the train one by one.

Task 2　Translate the following sentences into Chinese.

1. Keep your belongings in front of you as the train stations are crowded.
　_____

2. If you are traveling with children, keep an eye on them especially in large crowds.
　_____

3. Self-service hot water is available in the carriage. For safety reason, read the instruction before using the water dispensers.
　_____

4. Safety devices are marked in red only be used in emergency. Do not touch them to avoid any accident.
　_____

5. Don't get off the train before it fully stops. Be aware of the gap between the train and the platform.
　_____

Task 3　Fill in the blanks according to the Chinese meanings.

Broadcast Service

　　When a high-speed train is going to _____(停车), there will be broadcast _____(通知) that tells the passengers where they are going to arrive. Both Chinese and English are available, making you worry free about _____(错过) your _____(到达) station. During the other time of the whole trip, quiet and gentle music will accompany with you. _____(寻呼) service is available when there is someone in need.

Task 1 Complete the chart after discussing in groups.

- How to set up Alipay account?
- How to use Alipay to pay?
- How to transfer money in Alipay?

Try to introduce the Alipay instructions in English.

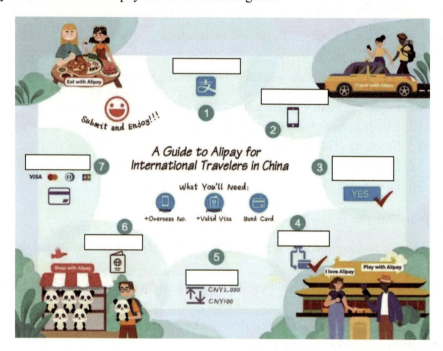

Task 2 Match the English in column A with their corresponding Chinese in column B.

A	B
Sign up with your phone	加载金额
Enter your passport info.	下载支付宝
Download Alipay	搜索旅游通行证
Load fund	输入银行卡信息
Search tour pass	选择国际版本
Enter your bank card info.	输入护照信息
Choose international version	转账
Transfer money	用手机号注册登录

Knowledge Stock

1. Main service, navigation & function of www.12306.cn

www.12306.cn has only Chinese language version and the language barrier could be the huge challenge for foreign travelers to use this site.

• Homepage: It contains everything about the main service, ranging from registration, remained ticket searching & booking, weather forecast, latest news, frequent asked questions about train tickets, etc.

• Ticket service: Travelers can choose to buy single & return tickets, cancel train tickets, change the destination, buy through trains to Hong Kong, check international train schedules and information and so on. How to buy tickets? First enter the departure city, arrival city, departure date and select the passenger type, and then "search". Updated China Train Schedules & Routes.

• Railway station service (车站服务): Here you can find station help for special passengers (like the old & who are difficult to take train), lost and found service, convenient train consignment service, customize pick-up and drop-off, railway station introduction.

• Train travel guide (出行指南): You can find many useful guides for taking train travel in China, including FAQs about booking, canceling train tickets, detailed introduction of train tickets and important regulations all passengers need to know.

• Information search (信息查询): You can check latest news, FAQs, credit information, ticket price, real-time weather, ticket agents, ticket checking gates, custom service contact number, and the earliest time to buy ticket.

2. High-speed train comfort quality—balance coin

This is no trick. This is for real. A nearly 10-minute video titled "High-speed train comfort quality—balance coin" has been widely circulated on Chinese video portals and social media.

In the video, all aboard a high-speed train hurtling across the Chinese landscape at the speed of 300 km/h, and the coin kept its balance on the window sill for nearly 8 minutes, promoting a surge in online viewers worldwide.

A Swedish man named Ola Von Koskull claimed he shot the video during his Chinese business trip and then uploaded it onto Youtube on March 14, 2015.

3. The materials for foreigners who want to use Alipay normally need

Foreigners who want to use Alipay normally need the following materials: Chinese phone number, Chinese bank account, passport and entry permit (or residence permit).

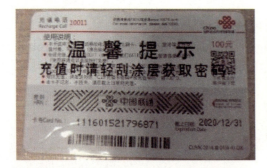

4. Facilities on High-speed Railway stations

Ticketing counters	售票处	Barrier-free facilities	无障碍设施
Information counters	询问处	Smoking room	吸烟室
Tourist services	旅客服务	Lost and found counter	失物认领处
Free station Wi-Fi	免费车站 Wi-Fi	Special assistance	特别协助
Free mobile device charging	免费流动装置充电设备	Car park	停车场
Business lounge	商务休息室	Luggage service	行李寄存处
Toilets/Nursing rooms	洗手间/育婴间	Luggage claim	行李托运处
Water dispensers	饮水机	Public open space	公共休息室

Section II
Station Service

Unit 3 Ticket Service

Goals

Be familiar with the expressions of train tickets;

Learn about ticketing information and the high-speed train seat classes;

Be able to help passengers buy train tickets;

Be able to help passengers refund tickets or change tickets.

Warming-up

Task 1 Match the expressions with the pictures.

Train number	Hard seat	Seat number
Departure time	Arrival station	Seat class
Departure platform	Ticket price	QR code
Departure station	Passenger's name	ID/Passport number

Task 2 Read the time in English.

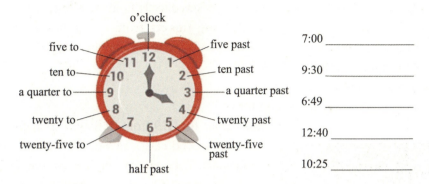

7:00 _____
9:30 _____
6:49 _____
12:40 _____
10:25 _____

The expressions above are for your reference.

Try to listen

The High-speed Railway broadcasting

Task 1 Listen carefully and fill in the blanks with what you hear.

Ladies and gentlemen, some trains will be _____ due to poor _____ condition. Please check the _____ board or ask station staff for _____ train schedules. We _____ for the inconvenience.

Task 2 Read the paragraph in Task 1 loudly and try to recite it.

Task 1 Retell the conversations below and imitate the pronunciation and intonation after listening to the recordings.

C 1 Consultation on ticket buying (购票信息咨询)

P=Passenger   S=Station staff

P: Can one passenger buy two tickets for the same train?
S: The Real-Name Ticket Policy admits that one passenger buys one ticket for the same train with the same departure date. ID cards or passports are valid identifications to issue the tickets.
P: What's the Real-Name Ticket Policy for?
S: It is to relieve the difficulty in buying tickets especially during the travel peaks. Passengers should buy tickets and get on board with their valid certificates.

25

P: Is there a service fee when buying a ticket?

S: There is no extra charge when purchasing tickets directly from the railway station. However, you need to wait in a queue. Buying tickets from an agency is much more convenient, therefore a certain amount of service fee may be charged.

C 2   At the ticket office (客票业务)

P=Passenger   T= Ticket agent

T: Good afternoon. What can I do for you?

P: I'd like to have three second class tickets for G19 from Beijing to Shanghai.

T: Sorry, second class seats of G19 are sold out. How about the first class seats or the next train G147's?

P: Do you mind if we discuss about it for a moment?... When will the next train depart?

T: It's 16:05, and the traveling time will be 33 minutes longer than G19. The ticket price is 533 yuan too.

P: All right, we'll take that train.

Task 2   Read and role-play the conversations in pairs.

C 1   Adult ticket

T: Good morning. What can I do for you?

P: Good morning. I want to buy a soft berth ticket from Tianjin to Shanghai the day after tomorrow.

T: Ok. When would you like to travel?

P: It's better after 9:00 a.m.

T: Is the ticket at 9:38 ok? The train number is G209 from Tianjin to Shanghai.

P: That's OK.

T: Do you prefer upper berth, middle berth or lower berth?

P: Lower berth, please.

T: All right. The fare is 510 yuan in all, please.

P: Here you are.

T: Here is your ticket and change. Please check it.

P: That's right.

T: Hope you have a good journey.

P: Thank you.

C 2   Student ticket

P: I want to buy a high-speed train student ticket to Chengdu for the day after tomorrow.

T: When would you like to travel?

P: I wish to leave in the afternoon.

T: Sorry, there are no tickets available for that time. How about some other time?

P: That's all right.

T: May I have your Citizen Identity Card and ID card?

P: Here you are my Citizen Identity Card and student ID card.

T: It is 310 yuan in all, please.

P: Here it is.

C 3   Refunding tickets

P: Excuse me.

T: Yes, what can I help you?

P: I bought two tickets from Beijing to Chongqing yesterday. But my wife is sick and we have to change our plan. May I get a refund for my tickets?

T: When is your train due to leave?

P: The day after tomorrow at 17:20.

T: I can help you with the refund. However, you have to pay 5 percent of the ticket price as a refund service charge.

P: That is fine. The price of each ticket is 630 yuan.

T: 5% of two tickets is 63 yuan. Here is your refund 1197 yuan.

C 4   Change ticket

P: Excuse me. May I get a refund for this ticket?

T: Let me look at your ticket first. Sorry, we can't refund it.

P: Why?

T: According to our policy, you can only refund your ticket before the train leaves.

P: What should I do?

T: You have no other choices. You could also change your ticket but it has to be within two hours after departure.

P: I see. Thank you.

Task 3   Situational practice

Situation 1: Suppose you are a ticket agent in a railway ticket office. A foreign passenger wants to buy a ticket. Before you can issue the ticket, you are required to get some information from the passenger such as destination, time or type of the ticket, etc. Make a conversation with your partner and try to practice it. You can refer to the following information.

- Where are you going?
- When would you like to travel?
- Please go to window No. 6 for student tickets.
- Children below 1.2 meters height don't have to pay.
- May I have your Citizen Identity Card and student ID card?

Situation 2: Suppose you are a clerk at the Inquiry office. A passenger needs your help for some information. Make a conversation with your partner and try to practice it. You can refer to the following information.

- How to help passengers to buy train tickets after working hour?
- How to use the self-service ticket facilities?
- When does the next train leave?
- How does he/she get to Shanghai?

- Which waiting room can he/she use?
- Where is the mother-child waiting room?

Task 4　Additional practice: phonetics (Back vowels)

1. Pronunciation methods

[u:]

发[u:]音的常见字母与字母组合有o、u、oo、ui、ou、ew。

发音方法：舌后部尽量抬起，双唇收圆并突出。

[ʊ]

发[ʊ]音的常见字母与字母组合有u、o、oo、ou。

发音方法：舌后部抬起，舌身后缩，比发[u:]时略低些，舌尖离开下齿。双唇收圆，稍突出。

[ɔ:]

发[ɔ:]音的常见字母与字母组合有al、or、au、aw、our、oor、augh、ough。

发音方法：舌后缩，舌后部抬起，舌尖不抵下齿，双唇收得更圆更小，并向前突出。

[ɒ]

发[ɒ]音的常见字母与字母组合有o、a。

发音方法：口张大，比发[ɔ:]时稍大，舌身尽量降低并后缩，舌后部比发[ɔ:]时抬得略低，双唇稍稍收圆。

[ɑ:]

发[ɑ:]音的常见字母与字母组合有a、ar、al、au。

发音方法：口张大，舌身压低并后缩，后舌稍隆起，舌尖不抵下齿，双唇稍收圆。

2. Read and practice

[u:]	tooth	who	soup	food	fruit	crew
[ʊ]	wood	pull	wolf	look	book	bull
[ɔ:]	daughter	water	strawberry	wall	horse	door
[ɒ]	want	fox	coffee	dog	long	watch
[ɑ:]	market	grass	arm	laugh	heart	half

Seat Classes on High-speed Trains

Tickets on high-speed trains are generally divided into second class seat, first class seat, business class seat, and VIP class seat. On some overnight D trains, soft sleeper and luxury soft sleeper are provided. Also on some D and G trains, standing-room-only tickets will be issued when all seats are sold out.

Facilities on these highballs are of high standard, similar to those on an airplane. The seats can be rotated towards the moving direction. The seatback can be adjusted to various angles, each passenger is offered a foldable small table, and electrical sockets are available in each row or compartment. Some even provide Wi-Fi service. In addition, dining and going to toilets will never be problems.

Business class seat has 3 seats per row (2+1), lie-flat seats. VIP class seat has 3 seats per row (2+1) or compartment seats which can in general recline. There are 4 seats per row (2+2) in first class seat compartment, and in second class seat, there are 5 seats per row (3+2), the sitting area is relatively small.

Soft sleeper contains a wider bunk bed in an enclosed cabin, two bunks to a side. The bunk beds are wider, and beddings are more comfortable than hard sleepers. There is more room for luggage storage as well in soft sleeper. Some soft sleepers have entertainment services with headphones and an LCD display for each bunk.

Deluxe soft sleeper is the top class sleeper that is only available in a few trains. The ticket is much more expensive than that of a soft sleeper. Each cabin has only two beds and its own bathroom. Some cabins even have showers.

Words and Expressions

generally	['dʒenrəli]	adv.	普遍地	rotate	[rəʊ'teɪt]	v.	旋转
divide	[dɪ'vaɪd]	v.	使分开	direction	[də'rekʃn]	n.	方向
luxury	['lʌkʃəri]	adj.	奢侈的	adjust	[ə'dʒʌst]	v.	调整
issue	[ɪʃu:]	v.	发布	angle	['æŋgl]	n.	角度
facility	[fə'sɪləti]	n.	设备	foldable	['fəʊldəbl]	adj.	可折叠的
highball	['haɪbɔ:l]	n.	铁路	premier	['premɪə]	adj.	首要的
bunk	[bʌŋk]	n.	铺位	deluxe	[dɪ'lʌks]	adj.	豪华的
LCD	[ˌel si:' di:]	n.	液晶显示屏				

Task 1 Choose the best answer.

1. Tickets on high-speed trains are generally divided into _____ types.
   A. three   B. four   C. five
2. The seats on high-speed train _____.
   A. can be rotated   B. can be adjusted   C. can be put down
3. Is there more room for luggage storage in soft sleeper?
   A. Yes, there is.   B. No, there is not.   C. Not mentioned.
4. How many seats are there per row in first class seat compartment?
   A. Not mentioned.   B. Four.   C. Five .
5. Which ticket is more expensive?
   A. Soft sleeper.   B. Deluxe soft sleeper.   C. Business class seat.

Task 2 Translate the following sentences into Chinese.

1. Tickets on high-speed trains are generally divided into second class seat, first class seat, business class seat, and VIP class seat.
_____

2. Facilities on these highballs are of high standard, similar to those on an airplane.
_____

3. Business class seat has 3 seats per row (2+1), lie-flat seats.
_____

4. Soft sleeper contains a wider bunk bed in an enclosed cabin, two bunks to a side.
_____

5. Deluxe soft sleeper is the top class sleeper that is only available in a few trains.
_____

Task 3 Fill in the blanks according to the Chinese meanings.

Real-Name Ticket Policy

From January 1, 2012, the _____(车票实名制) applies to all trains in China, aim to relieve the difficulty in buying tickets and effectively stop scalpers who profit a lot in trading rail tickets especially during the _____(春运) rush every year. Original _____(有效证件) become a MUST for China High-speed Railway _____(预定车票), collecting, altering and canceling.

It is allowed to buy one ticket per valid identity document. Your Identity Document number will be printed on the ticket. When boarding the train, you should _____(出示你的火车票) and your valid Identity Document together to the steward.

Group Work

Task 1 Look at the flow chart and discuss in groups how to buy train tickets online (on www.12306.cn). Make a performance in English according to the ticket sales procedure within each group.

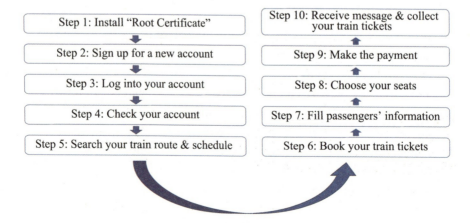

Task 2 Match the English in column A with their corresponding Chinese in column B.

A	B
Book tickets	车票有效期
Round-trip ticket	学生票
Student ticket	卧铺票
Child ticket	退票
Berth ticket	二等座
Economy-class seat	儿童票
Get a refund for a ticket	学生票
Cancellation charge	退票手续费
The valid time of a ticket	订票

Knowledge Stock

1. The knowledge about selling tickets with pictures and words

Internet ticket terminal
互联网取票终端

Railway ticketing system
铁路售票系统

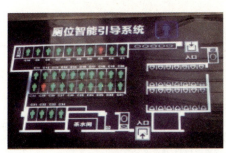

Smart-toilets system
厕位智能引导系统

Train timetable
列车时刻表

Ticket office
售票处

Ticket counter
人工售票窗口

Ticket agent
车站售票员

Automatic ticket
自动售票机

2. China train schedules and routes

Railway lines (From/To)	Train number	Timetable	Duration	Tickets (RMB)	Major stops
Beijin-Shanghai	G1, G3, G5, G7, G9, G11, G13, G15, G17, G21...	6:43-21:23	4h 18min-12h 7min	Second class: 553.0 First class: 933.0 Business class: 1748.0	Nanjing
Beijing-Xi'an	G87, G89, G651, G671, G429, G661...	6:05-18:55	4h 20min-6h 2min	Second class: 515.5 First class: 824.5 Business class: 1627.5	Zhengzhou East
Beijing-Tianjin	C2001, C2017, G5, G261, G105, G23, C2211, C2043...	6:05-18:55	31min-1h 8min	Second class: 54.5 First class: 94.5 Business class: 174.5	—
Beijing-Guangzhou	G65, G67, G69, G71, G79, G901, G903...	7:27-20:35	8h 1min-10h 18min	Second class: 862.0 First class: 1380.0 Business class: 2724.0	Wuhan Changsha Zhengzhou

Railway lines (From/To)	Train number	Timetable	Duration	Tickets (RMB)	Major stops
Beijing-Chengdu	G89, G307, G571	6:53-9:38	7h 48min-10h 4min	Second class: 778.5 First class: 1246.0 Business class: 2417.0	Xi'an North
Beijing-Changsha	G65, G83, G505, G65, G67, G403, G485...	7:03-15:40	5h 38min-7h 38min	Second class: 649.0 First class: 1038.0 Business class: 2050.0	Zhengzhou Wuhan
Beijing-Hangzhou	G19, G31, G33, G39, G45, G167, G163...	7:15-19:04	4h 18min-6h 42min	Second class: 538.5 First class: 907.0 Business class: 1701.0	Nanjing Jinan Tianjin
Beijing-Chongqing	G309, G571	8:23-09:22	11h 34min-12h 11min	Second class: 924.5 First class: 1455.5 Business class: 2814.0	Shijiazhuang Zhengzhou Yichang

Unit 3 Ticket Service

Unit 4 Security Check

Goals

Be familiar with the prohibited items;
Learn about limited items on high-speed trains;
Learn about the security check procedure;
Learn to cope with some special things during the security check.

Warming-up

Try to think

Task 1 Match the words and expressions with the pictures.

Ammunition	Magnetized	Oxidising	Firearms
Police weapons	Blunt material	Poisons	Radioactive
Corrosives	Knives	Flammable explosives	Sharp material

1._____   2._____   3._____   4._____   5._____   6._____

7._____   8._____   9._____   10._____   11._____   12._____

34

Task 2 Do you know any other forbidden or limited items? Please list them as many as possible, then fill in the quantity of the following limited items.

1. Lighter: _____ ordinary fighters at most.
2. Cigarette: _____ cartons(盒) of cigarettes at most.
3. Safety match: _____ small boxes at most.
4. Nail polish(指甲油), delusterant(去光剂) or hair dye(染发剂) shall no exceed _____ mL.
5. Insecticide(杀虫剂), air freshener, hair fixture(发胶), mousses(摩丝) shall no exceed _____ mL.

Try to listen

The High-speed Railway broadcasting

Task 1 Listen carefully and fill in the blanks with what you hear.

Ladies and gentlemen, poisonous and flammable _____ are not allowed in the train. If you have any, please _____ the attendants immediately. The extinguisher is available at the end of each carriage. The first window at the end of each carriage is the emergency _____. The _____ button can only be used in an emergency, and please do not touch it otherwise. _____ is strictly prohibited during the whole trip. Violators will be punished according to the *Regulations on the Administration of Railway Safety*.

Task 2 Read the paragraph in Task 1 loudly and try to recite it.

Conversations

Task 1 Retell the conversations below and imitate the pronunciation and intonation after listening to the recordings.

C 1 **Identity check for a foreigner** (外籍人士验票)

P=Passenger   S=Station staff

S: Please show me your ticket and passport, please.

P: Here you go.

S: The name on the passport does not match the name on your ticket.

P: Is that right? Could you please double check?

S: Hmm... Maybe you gave me a wrong ticket.

P: Oh, sorry, that's my husband's. (After exchanging the ticket with her husband) Is this right now?

S: Ok. This way, please.

C 2 Security check requirements (自觉接受安检)

I=Inspector   P=Passenger

I : Good afternoon, Madam. Security check, please.

P : I only have a jacket in my bag.

I : Every luggage needs to go through the X-ray, and everyone needs to go through security scanners. This is the rule of the station.

P : No problem. Is it ok to keep wallet, phone and passport in the pants pocket?

I : Yes. Please lay your bag on the belt.

P : Sure, thanks.

I : Madam, please wait a moment. Is there half a bottle of water in your bag?

P : Yeah. Anything wrong?

I : You must empty the bottle or have a sip yourself to prove that is not harmful?

P : Sure. (After drinking) Well, I don't know why you're so strict.

I : Safety is our top priority. We must take our security checks seriously.

P : I see. Thank you.

I : My pleasure. Have a nice day!

Word Tips

X-ray	['eksreɪ]	v.	用X射线拍摄检查	pants	[pænts]	n.	裤子
scanner	['skænə(r)]	n.	扫描仪器	sip	[sɪp]	n.	一小口

Task 2   Read and role-play the conversations in pairs.

C 1

I=Inspector   P=Passenger

I : Excuse me madam, wait a moment. Please unpack your suitcase.

P : Why?

I : We suspect that there are some prohibited items in your suitcase.

P : That's impossible.

I : Madam, it is strictly prohibited to carry more than 120 mL hair dye on the train. And you are carrying a bottle of 200 mL hair dye. This has exceeded the maximum amount allowed.

P : Sorry, I don't know this before.

I : That is ok. However, you can't carry this with you on the train.

P : Ok, I'll discard this.

I : Thank you. Please remember to collect your items at the end.

C 2

I : Please stay in line and wait for your turn.

P : Ok.

I : Excuse me sir, what do you have in your pocket? You aren't allowed to carry a gun into the station.

P : Oh, I'm sorry it's my son's toy gun.

I : Let me have a check. (After checking) Ok, anything else in your pocket?

P: Nothing.

I : Sir, knives should be checked. You are not allowed to carry them on a train.

P: Oh, sorry. I forgot about this. What should I do?

I : We could keep it for you. But you must come back in one month or you can discard it.

P: Let me discard it.

I : Thank you for your cooperation.

C 3

I : Excuse me, is this your bag?

P: Yes.

I : What's that?

P: A cat.

I : It is prohibited to be taken onto to the train.

P: Oh, sorry. I don't know the regulations. What should I do?

I : You can check it at the luggage office, but you should have a quarantine certification.

P: I see. Thanks.

I : You are welcome.

Word Tips

| prohibit | [prə'hɪbɪt] | v. | 禁止 | quarantine | ['kwɒrəntiːn] | n. | 检疫 |
| regulation | [ˌreɡju'leɪʃn] | n. | 规则 | certification | [ˌsɜːtɪfɪ'keɪʃn] | n. | 证明 |

Task 3 Situational practice

Situation 1: Suppose you are a security inspector in the station. A passenger is a blindman, carrying a guide dog. He forgot his ID. You offer help to him. How does he go through the security check? Make a conversation with your partner and try to practice it.

Situation 2: Suppose you are a security inspector in the station. A passenger is a college student, carrying a durian(榴梿). She wants to take a high-speed train from Shanghai to Beijing for sightseeing in summer vacation. You offer help to her. How does she go through the security check? Make a conversation with your partner and try to practice it.

Task 4 Additional practice: phonetics (Diphthongs)

1. Pronunciation methods

[ɪə]

[ɪə]是双元音，发[ɪə]音的常见字母与字母组合有ea、ear、eer、ier、ere。

发音方法：从[ɪ]音很快滑向[ə]音。前面的[ɪ]发得较清楚，后面的[ə]较弱。双唇由扁平变成半开。

[eə]

[eə]是双元音，发[eə]音的常见字母与字母组合有are、air、ear、eir、ere。

发音方法：从[e]音很快滑向[ə]音。发间时舌端抵下齿，前舌略抬起，双唇半开。

[ʊə]

[ʊə]是双元音，发[ʊə]音的常见字母与字母组合有our、ure、ua、oor。

发音方法：发音时，嘴唇从收圆到半开。发好这个音的关键是：首先要把[ʊ]音发足，然后滑向[ə]音。

2. Read and practice

[ɪə]	cheer	hear	dear	tear	beer	deer
[eə]	prepare	hair	square	there	theirs	wear
[ʊə]	February	poor	tourist	tour	sure	usually

Security Check Required for All

To ensure a safe environment in both stations and trains, all persons must undergo security checks before they are admitted into the station for boarding. After you arrive at the right train station and have your ticket(s) ready, line up for the security check. There will be conductors checking the tickets. A moving conveyor belt and a metal detection door are installed at the entrance for security check. Please remove liquids from your bags as they will be checked separately.

For foreign visitors, you could go through the manual checking points. As there are several queues for manual checking process, you can join in any one of them. Show your ticket and valid passport to the staff and face to the camera to recognize your image, and then, he/she would seal on your ticket to show you pass the real-name recognition. At some comparatively smaller train stations, the staff would directly verify your real look and the image on your passport to go through the step.

At some stations, security staff may limit the number of passengers going through security check at any one time. This is to ensure passengers ahead of you have enough time to collect their belongings.

The following items are DANGEROUS and MUST NOT be carried or consigned: flammable or explosive materials, poison, poisonous materials and harmful liquids, radioactive or magnetic items, weapons, or anything that resembles or emulates a weapon.

Please pay close attention to safety notices at your station. Passengers who break the law are liable for legal consequences, and may be prosecuted.

Words and Expressions

English	IPA	Part	Chinese	English	IPA	Part	Chinese
ensure	[ɪn'ʃʊə(r)]	v.	确保	flammable	['flæməbl]	adj.	易燃的
undergo	[ˌʌndə'gəʊ]	v.	经历	explosive	[ɪk'spləʊsɪv]	adj.	易爆炸的
admit	[æd'mɪt]	v.	准许……进入	liquid	['lɪkwɪd]	n.	液体
conveyor	[kən'veɪə(r)]	n.	传送带	radioactive	[ˌreɪdiəʊ'æktɪv]	adj.	放射性的
detection	[dɪ'tekʃn]	n.	探测	magnetic	[mæg'netɪk]	adj	有磁性的
manual	['mænjuəl]	adj.	用手操作的	resemble	[rɪ'zembl]	v.	看起来像
valid	['vælɪd]	adj.	有效的	emulate	['emjuleɪt]	v.	仿真
seal	[si:l]	v.	盖章	liable	['laɪəbl]	adj	（法律上）负有责任的
recognition	[ˌrekəg'nɪʃn]	n.	识别				
verify	['verɪfaɪ]	v.	核实	consequence	['kɒnsɪkwəns]	n.	结果
image	['ɪmɪdʒ]	n.	形象	prosecute	['prɒsɪkju:t]	v.	起诉
consign	[kən'saɪn]	v.	托运	checking point			检测点

Task 1 Choose the best answer.

1. A security check doesn't happen _____.
   A. before entering the station building
   B. before entering the waiting hall
   C. after entering the waiting hall
2. Foreign visitors could pass through the identity check by _____.
   A. the automatic checking   B. no checking   C. the manual checking
3. At some smaller train stations, would the staff directly verify your real look and the image on your passport?
   A. No, he /she would not.   B. Yes, he /she would.   C. Not mentioned.
4. The following articles can be carried on the train except _____.
   A. fireworks   B. water   C. lighters
5. What does the security check include?
   A. Luggage check.   B. Identification check.   C. Both of them.

Task 2 Translate the following sentences into Chinese.

1. To ensure a safe environment in both stations and trains, all persons must undergo security checks before they are admitted into the station for boarding.
   _____

2. After you arrive at the right train station and have your ticket(s) ready, line up for the security check.
   _____

3. As there are several queues for manual checking process, you can join in any one of them.
   _____

4. Show your ticket and valid passport to the staff and face to the camera to recognize your image, and then, he/she would seal on your ticket to show you pass the real-name recognition.

_____

5. Please pay close attention to safety notices at your station.

_____

Task 3　Fill in the blanks according to the Chinese meanings.

How to Get to Train Station

The first thing you should do after obtaining your ticket is checking the train station and _____(开车时间) and other details. Check the _____(交通路线) and available way to get there. _____(出租车) is the most convenient way for large luggage carriers. And usually you can also _____(乘坐地铁), bus to get there unless you have plenty of time. Please remember to arrive at the waiting hall at least 30 minutes ahead of departure and leave enough time to _____(通过) security, check and locate the right _____(检票口).

Group Work

Task 1　Look at the workflow of security check and discuss in groups what the security check services are. Make a performance in English according to the procedure of the security check services within each group.

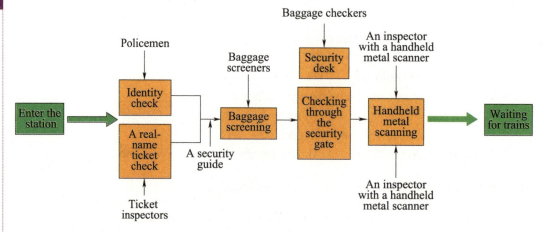

Task 2　Arrange the following sentences in logical order.

A. Search carry-on or checked luggage by hand when it is suspected to contain prohibited items such as weapons.

B. Perform pat-down or hand-held wand searches of passengers.

C. Check passengers' tickets and personal documentation to ensure that they are valid.

D. Direct passengers to areas where they can put their luggage after identity check is complete.

E. Inspect carry-on items, using X-ray viewing equipment, to determine whether items contain objects that warrant further investigation.

F. The security check is complete.

G. Direct passengers to security gate for body scanning.

Correct order: _____

1. Some acceptable travel documents on high-speed train
- Valid passports
- Resident identity card
- Mainland travel permit for Hong Kong and Macau residents
- PRC exit/entry permit for traveling to and from Hong Kong and Macau
- Mainland travel permit for Taiwan residents

2. Things prohibited and limited to bring on train
- Items forbidden to take on train-what you can't bring on train

Wherever you depart, any destination you arrive, the following all items are strictly prohibited to be taken abroad.

(1) Weapons: guns, bullets, sporting rifles, firefighting guns, animation guns, popguns, and other samples and imitations of weaponry.

(2) Knives: daggers, flicking knives, kitchen knives, fruit knives, axes, spontoons, defibrillators, bows and arrows, etc.

(3) Live Animals: pets, poultry (except guide dogs) and any living creature; and any goods with strong unpleasant smell.

(4) Explosives: bombs, flare, signal flares, tear gas, explosives, dynamites, fireworks, firecrackers, and any duplicates of above articles.

(5) Inflammables: oxygen (except bagged medical oxygen), hydrogen, methane, ethane, butane, natural gas, carbon oxide, liquefied petroleum gas, and other compressed and liquefied gas; gasoline, kerosene, diesel, ethyl alcohol, else combustible liquid and etc.

(6) Dangerous Goods: poisons (cyanide, arsenic, selenium, and highly toxic chemicals); corrosives (vitriol, hydrochloric acid, accumulator, mercury and etc.); radioactive materials, infectious articles (AIDS, HBV, anthrax, tubercle bacillus...).

(7) Magnetized items.

- Items limited to take on train

Passengers can carry the following items on train within the limited quantity. Any case exceeding the maximum restriction will be handled according to the relevant national regulations.

(1) Nail polish, delusterant, hair dye shall no exceed 20 mL.

(2) Insecticide, air freshener, hair fixture, mousses and pressure vessels (such as sunscreen spray, deodorant spray...) shall no exceed 120 mL.

(3) Safety match: 2 small boxes at most.

(4) Lighter: 2 ordinary fighters at most.

(5) Cigarette: 50 cartons of cigarettes at most.

• Note

(1) Once found any objects prohibited before boarding, passengers will be rejected checking in at the train station;

(2) If the dangerous goods are discovered on train, passenger have to hand over them to train stuff for further proper disposal;

(3) Blind passengers carrying guide dogs are required to show necessary proof, including valid ID, certificate of disabled, quarantine certificate and so on.

3. Items prohibited to take on train during the phase of the outbreak of Coronavirus

During the phase of the outbreak of Coronavirus, passengers who will take a train travel should be noticed that the following items are NOT allowed to bring with you to your train.

• No 84 disinfectant, sanitizer, and bleach

The alcohol concentration of 84 disinfectant, sanitizer, and bleach usually reach 75% or more.

As you know, when a passenger on the train splashes the sanitizer on the hands, tables and chairs, it is possible to ignite or even explode the spark on the air.

For safety concern, China Rail prohibits any passenger to take such sanitizer onto the train.

• No pressure tanks

Pressure tanks that over 120 mL with inflammable constituent are NOT allowed to bring onto the train. For example:

(1) Sunscreen spray;

(2) Water spray;

(3) Mosquito repellent spray;

(4) Fixature;

(5) Perfume;

(6) Shaving foam.

4. Consign your luggage—express service

Passengers going to take luggage in super large size or inconvenient to carry may choose the luggage and parcel transportation service by railway if the departure and destination stations both have luggage service. Normal train passenger is limited to check luggage one time only with a valid ticket, while the disabled ticket owner can make the consignment many times.

Important tips for railway luggage consignment:

(1) Suitcase, trolley bag, and handbag and so on personal luggage should be tightly and completely packed for railway transportation.

(2) The total weight shall no exceed 50 kg/110 lb. If not, the extra part will be paid with a large surcharge.

(3) Senders must write down the detailed information clearly and accurately, including the name, address of the sender and receiver.

(4) The checked luggage is charged according to fixed unit price and exact weight.

(5) Senders can collect the luggage and parcel with check receipt once receive the notice. The luggage will be kept without charge for only 3 days.

Unit 5　Waiting Service

Goals

Be able to answer questions about waiting service;
Be able to give direction and position to passengers;
Be able to help passengers when they are in trouble;
Master useful expressions for luggage service.

Task 1　Match the expressions with the pictures.

LED screen　　　Porter service　　　Luggage deposit
Waiting hall　　　Dining area　　　　Business class lounge

1._____　　2._____

43

3. _____   4. _____

5. _____   6. _____

Task 2 Answer the questions.

1. Do you know any guidance marks in High-speed Railway station? Please list them as many as possible.

2. What other services can be provided for passengers in the waiting hall?

The High-speed Railway broadcasting

Task 1 Listen carefully and fill in the blanks with what you hear.

Dear passengers, please do not lie on the chairs or _____ while waiting for the train because of the _____ passenger flow at the station. For other passengers' _____, please take your luggage _____ from the seats and leave it on the floor. Thank you for your cooperation. Have a nice _____!

Task 2 Read the paragraph in Task 1 loudly and recite it.

Conversations

Task 1 Retell the conversations below and imitate the pronunciation and intonation after listening to the recordings.

C 1 **Dinning in stations** (车站餐饮)

P=Passenger S=Station staff

S: Good morning Sir. What can I do for you?

P: I'm hungry. Is there any restaurants in the station?

S: Huangshanbei Railway Station is small. There are only a few restaurants here.

P: I see. Any recommendations?

S: Hmm... For local Chinese food, I strongly recommend Huangshan traditional food such as Soy Braised Mandarin Fish (臭鳜鱼) and hairy tofu (毛豆腐).

P: Anything else?

S: For western-style food, there are KFC and McDonald's inside the station.

P: Ok, thanks.

S: You are welcome.

Word Tips

recommendation	[ˌrekəmen'deɪʃn]	n.	推荐	soy	[sɔɪ]	n.	大豆
braise	[breɪz]	v.	炖;煨	Mandarin Fish	['mændərɪn fɪʃ]		鳜鱼

C 2 Looking for a porter (寻找行李搬运工)

S: Sir, may I help you?

P: Do you know where I get a porter?

S: The men wearing red hats are the porters. They can help you to carry your luggage onto the train.

P: Hmm... I don't see any.

S: I'll get one for you.

P: Thanks. Is the service free of charge?

S: Unfortunately, it is not free.

P: What's the charge?

S: It depends on how many pieces of luggage you have. You can get more information from the porters.

P: I see. Thank you.

S: Sure.

Word Tips

redcap	['redkæp]	n.	行李搬运员	unfortunately	[ʌn'fɔːtʃənətli]	adv.	遗憾地

Task 2　Read and role-play the conversations in pairs.

C 1

P: Excuse me. I want to have my luggage checked in.

S: Sorry, there's no such service available for CRH. But you can check your luggage at the luggage office for normal trains.

P: Thank you. Where is the luggage office?

S: It's on the first floor. It's only five minutes' walk from here. You will need to fill a form at the luggage office and sign at the bottom.

P: Thank you for your reminding.

S: My pleasure.

C 2

P: Good morning, I'd like to claim my luggage. Here's the consignment note.

S: Please wait for a moment while I check your information on the computer. Ok, these are five pieces of luggage under your name including a suitcase and four traveling bags, right?

P: Yes, thank you.

S: My pleasure.

C 3

P: Excuse me, where is the ladies' room?

S: Take the elevator to the second floor. Once you get out of the elevator, turn left. The ladies' room is right on your left.

P: To the second floor and turn left?

S: Right. you won't miss it.

P: But where is the elevator?

S: It's around the corner.

Task 3　Situational practice

Situation 1: Suppose you are a staff member in the station. You see a pair of foreign couple, carrying three kids. One of kids wants to go to the toilet. One wants to play. How do you give some advice for them? Make a conversation with your partner and try to practice it.

Situation 2: Suppose you are a redcap in the station. You see a passenger, carrying some heavier luggage. She requires porter service. You offer help to her. Make a conversation with your partner and try to practice it.

Task 4　Additional practice: phonetics (Diphthongs)

1. Pronunciation methods

[ai]

发[ai]音的常见字母与字母组合有i、y、ie、ye、igh。

发音方法：先发[a]音，然后滑向[i]音。舌尖抵住下齿。发此音时要把[a]音发足，注意从开到合的滑动。

[ei]

发[ei]音的常见字母与字母组合有a、ai、ay、eigh。

发音方法：先发[e]音，然后滑向[i]音。双唇稍扁，口形从半开到合。

[ɔi]

发[ɔi]音的常见字母与字母组合有oi、oy。

发音方法：发好这个音的关键是首先要把后元音[ɔ]发足，然后滑向[i]音。发音时双唇从圆到扁，口形从开到合。

[əʊ]

发[əʊ]音的常见字母与字母组合有o、oa、ou、ow。

发音方法：它由元音[ə]滑向后元音[ʊ]，舌位由半低到高，口形由半开到小，双唇由扁平到圆。注意将音发足。

[aʊ]

发[aʊ]音的常见字母与字母组合有ou、ow。

发音方法：由[a]滑向[ʊ]，舌位由低到高，口形由大到小，双唇逐渐合圆并稍向前突出。

2. Read and practice

[ai]	high	tiger	fly	pie	buy	write
[ei]	weight	name	pay	train	wait	today
[ɔi]	spoil	boil	coin	enjoy	noise	toilet
[əʊ]	soul	over	soap	window	row	goat
[aʊ]	about	trousers	blouse	cloud	clown	town

Reading

Facilities and Service in the Waiting Hall

Station facilities usually consist of one or two squares, a terminal building and a station yard. The station building is a main hall of the High-speed Railway station, where with a valid ticket, you can enter the station hall. After entering the station, read the LED screen to find your waiting hall. In the most railway stations, the waiting hall is located in the first or second floor or both. Some railway station has a big waiting hall in one floor, while others may have several separated waiting halls. The boarding/disembarking platform is always located in the first floor or the first floor ground, so you need to get down from the waiting hall to the platform usually. The subway station is always located below the platform floor. Follow the direction indicator, you will find the parking lot, bus station and exit easily. Most of the railway stations, especially the recently-built High-speed Railway stations are more user-friendly. They not only offer necessary facilities to meet basic needs of passengers, but also provide helpful service.

LED screen: After you enter the station hall, you will firstly see a big LED screen, which show the present days' train information, like train number, departure time, arrival station, corresponding waiting hall, corresponding checking gate, etc.

Seats: All the waiting halls are equipped with a number of seats, and some of them are comfortably cushioned. Please find your checking gate firstly and take a seat nearby. In the peak seasons (May Day, Chinese National Day and Spring Festival), the seat will in short supply.

Stores and markets: There are markets selling some snacks, drinks or some local souvenirs, but the price is higher than the outside markets. Some railway stations also have one book store.

Restaurant: Dining area is located in the waiting hall floor or the upper interlayer. You can find some fast-food restaurants like KFC, McDonald's or Dicos and some Chinese restaurants which sell noodles, dumplings, steamed stuffed buns, etc.

Luggage deposit: If it's far from your departure time and you want to walk around, you could deposit your luggage in Left Luggage Office. The charge varies on different railway stations-some charge you according to the weight and some according to the number or volume.

Inquiry counter: There is an inquiry counter in every railway station. Some staffs are able to speak simple English and you can turn them for help when you encounter some problems.

Business class lounge: There is at least one business class lounge in every railway station. If you book a Business Seat, you are able to wait in the business class lounge where the environment is much quiet and there are some snacks and drinks provided.

Smoking area: If you are a smoker, go to the smoking area when you need. The smoking area is generally equipped near the toilets in the waiting hall. In most railway stations, the English sign will lead you to this area.

Porter service: Many railway stations offer paid porter service. The porter are called Red Cap because they were redcap and waistcoat. They can help you carry your luggage from the station hall to your carriage of your train, or from the arrival platform to your car or taxi. This service will be charged differently according to different railway stations.

Words and Expressions

terminal	['tɜmɪnl]	adj.	终端的	corresponding	[ˌkɒrə'spɒndɪŋ]	n.	对应的
valid	['vælɪd]	adj.	有效的	equipped	[ɪ'kwɪpt]	v.	装备
railway	['reɪlweɪ]	n.	铁路	deposit	[dɪ'pɒzɪt]	v.	存放
separated	['sepəreɪtɪd]	adj.	分开的	counter	['kaʊntə]	n.	柜台
boarding	['bɔːdɪŋ]	v.	登车	lounge	[laʊndʒ]	n.	休息室
peak	[piːk]	n.	顶点	disembark	[ˌdɪsɪm'bɑːk]	v.	下车
indicator	['ɪndɪkeɪtə]	n.	标识	station yard			站场
facilities	[fə'sɪlɪtɪz]	n.	设备	LED screen			电子显示屏
departure	[dɪ'pɑːtʃə]	n.	离开				

Task 1 Choose the best answer.

1. After entering the station, how can you find your waiting hall?
   A. By reading the LED screen.
   B. By asking others.
   C. By inquiring friends.
2. What does the stores in the waiting hall selling?
   A. Local souvenirs.　　　B. Clothes.　　　C. Ticket.
3. Where can you put your luggage temporary in the waiting hall?
   A. Information counter.　　B. Luggage deposit.　　C. Waiting hall.
4. If you encounter some problems in the station whom can you turn for help?
   A. Clerk in the ticket office.
   B. Tourist.
   C. Staff in the inquiry counter.
5. Where is the boarding or disembarking platform locate?
   A. The first floor.　　B. The second floor.　　C. The third floor.

Task 2 Translate the following sentences into Chinese.

1. Some railway station has a big waiting hall in one floor, while others may have several separated waiting halls.
_____

2. Most of the railway stations, especially the recently-built High-speed Railway stations are more user-friendly.
_____

3. There are markets selling some snacks, drinks or some local souvenirs, but the price is higher than the outside markets.
_____

4. If it's far from your departure time and you want to walk around, you could deposit your luggage in Left Luggage Office.
_____

5. The porter are called Red Cap because they were redcap and waistcoat.
_____

Task 3 Fill in the blanks according to the Chinese meanings.

Guide at Train Station

A train station often offers many _____(设施) and services for _____(顾客的方便). Except the ticket counters, there are many automatic ticket machines and e-ticket pick-up machines in and near the ticket office. For _____(娱乐), you can find some small shops, restaurants, _____(银行提款机) around the train station, nearby the entrance or inside the waiting hall and special facilities for disabled person, mother and _____(婴儿) at train station. KFC, McDonald's and other western style snack bars can be found in lots of big train stations.

Task 1　Collect information about the station services at railway station in groups and make a report about the introduction of these services in English within each group. You can refer to the following chart.

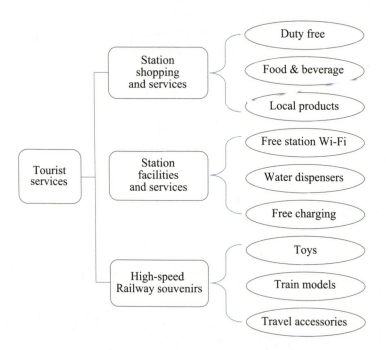

Task 2　Match the English in column A with their corresponding Chinese in column B.

A	B
Tourist services	当地特产
High-speed Railway souvenirs	免费车站Wi-Fi
Duty free	免费充电
Local products	火车模型
Free station Wi-Fi	旅行用品
Free charge	车站服务
Water dispensers	中铁快运
Train models	高铁纪念品
Travel accessories	旅客服务
China Railway Express	免税店

Knowledge Stock

1. Eight most beautiful High-speed Railways in China

Below are 8 magnificent High-speed Railways which have not only fabulous landscape on route, but also connect the most beautiful destinations in China.

- Shanghai to Kunming High-speed Railway—the Spring Train
- Urumqi to Lanzhou High-speed Railway—the Ancient Silk Road Train
- Guangzhou Guilin Guiyang High-speed Railway—the Karst Landscape Train
- Xi'an Chengdu High-speed Railway—the Panda Train
- Xiamen Wuyishan Yellow Mountain High-speed Railway—the Landscape Train
- Shanghai Hong Kong High-speed Railway—the Leisure Coastal Train
- Hainan Island Circular Train
- Harbin Ice Festival Train

2. Four colors of Chinese trains

- 绿皮车：green-skinned train 普通列车 (a traditional nickname for old-style trains)
- 红皮车：red-skinned train 快速列车 (K字头)
- 蓝皮车：blue-skinned train 特快列车 (T字头)
- 白皮车：white-skinned train 直达特快列车

3. Carry-on luggage allowance

Passengers who have already bought train tickets are allowed to carry personal luggage to the trains free of charge, without limitation of amount and types. And a brief guide (in Chinese version only) about train carry-on luggage size and weight, and other useful information are printed on the back of the train ticket for your consideration.

In order to offer you the best ideas for packing and a hassle-free boarding and train travel experience, we are presenting the most specific details about the hand luggage policy for you. Just remember, normally you can take as much as you can, as long as you can hand it independently and find right places to place it. Usually, neither the size nor the weight will be checked specifically.

• Carry-on luggage weight allowance

The free carry-on luggage weight allowance for every passenger is slightly different from various types of train tickets.

(1) For each child (children-ticket holders & who are free of admission): max.10 kg/22lb;
(2) For each adult: max. 20 kg/44 lb;
(3) For each diplomat: max. 35 kg/77 lb.

• Carry-on luggage size allowance

Each piece passengers can take on aboard has theoretically limitation of dimensions, a sum of the length, width and height. Personal luggage, suitcases, handbags and boxes included, are free to take into the carriage without exceeding the outside measurement. That way you can store your luggage appropriately in somewhere on the train.

(1) For normal train: max. 160 cm/63 in (length × width × height);
(2) For high-speed train: max.130 cm/51 in (length × width × height);
(3) The rod-shaped item: shall not exceed 200 cm/79 in (length).

Note well: The above carry-on luggage allowance does not apply to folding wheelchair for the disabled. In other words, one can take the folding wheelchairs on as extra luggage, and the weight and volume of the folding wheelchair are not included in the carry-on luggage rules.

Unit 6 Ticket Checking

Goals

Be familiar with the facilities of ticket-checking;
Master the words and expressions about ticket checking;
Understand the procedures of ticket checking;
Learn to offer help to passengers at boarding gate.

Warming-up

Try to think

Task 1 Match the words and expressions with the pictures.

Automatic checking machine   Second generation ID card
Interphone/Walkie-talkie   Magnetic ticket
Boarding gate   Ticket clipper

1._____

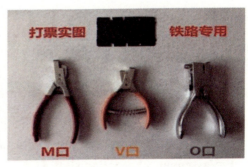

2._____

3. _____

4. _____

5. _____
6. _____

Task 2   What do you know about the automatic checking machine?

Try to listen

The High-speed Railway broadcasting

Task 1   Listen carefully and fill in the blanks with what you hear.

　　Ladies and gentlemen, attention please. It is now the _____ time for train G6007 from Changsha to Guangzhou. Passengers for train _____ please get your _____ and _____ ready to check in at gate _____. Thank you for your cooperation.

Task 2   Read the paragraph in Task 1 loudly and try to recite it.

Task 1   Retell the conversations below and imitate the pronunciation and intonation after listening to the recordings.

　　C 1   Check the ticket and respond to passengers' inquiries (检票并回复旅客询问)
　　P=Passenger   S=Station staff
　　P: Do I check in for the train G404 to Shanghai here?

S: Yes, can I have your tickets and ID card, please?

P: Here you go.

S: Thanks. This way, please.

P: Why?

S: The other gate leads to a different platform.

P: Sorry, I don't know.

S: That is ok.

P: What is the platform for the train G404?

S: Planform 6. Please follow this way to the platform.

P: Thank you very much.

S: You are welcome. Have a good trip.

C 2 Help passengers go through the ticket checking machine (如何通过安检口)

P: Hello, the automatic gate won't open. Could you please help me with it?

S: Please step back and try again.

P: It still does not work.

S: Ok. Please take you ticket, stand behind the yellow line and try again.

P: What should I do with the ticket?

S: You can insert your ticket in the slot here. If the machine successfully checks you in, your ticket will pop out from a separate slot on the top of the machine.

P: Ok, the gate is open.

S: You can now take your ticket and pass the gate.

P: Thank you.

S: It's my pleasure.

Word Tips

| insert | [ɪnˈsɜːt] | v. | 插入 | slot | [slɒt] | n. | 狭槽 |

Task 2 Read and role-play the conversations in pairs.

C 1

P: May I have your ticket please?

S: Yes, here you are.

P: Oh, I am afraid that you are taking the wrong train. This is G203, not G201.

S: Sorry. When will G201 leave?

P: G201 departs at 18:50. And the ticket checking will start at 18:35.

S: Got it. Thanks.

P: You are welcome.

C 2

S: Ticket, please.

P: Ok, here it is.

S: Thanks. Your ticket is for the train G135 yesterday. It is invalid now.

P: Oh, my god! I remember the date wrong.

S: Sorry to know it.

P: What should I do now?

S: You need to buy a new ticket.

P: Ok, I will buy a new one with my mobile phone.

S: Good idea. You can use your ID card for boarding.

C 3

(A passenger is running to the boarding gate in a hurry.)

P: This is my ticket, please check it.

S: I am very sorry but the check-in is stopped. The gate is closed, and I can't let you in.

P: Why? The ticket shows the train leaves at 10:30, and there are still three minutes left.

S: Sir, according to the regulations, ticket checking stops 3 minutes before train's departure time.

P: What should I do next?

S: You missed this train. Please change your ticket at the ticket office.

C 4

P: Excuse me. What is the difference between the blue ticket and the red paper type?

S: There is no big difference. That red tickets need to be checked manually, while blue ones can be checked by automatic ticket checking machines.

P: I see. Thanks.

S: Please keep your ticket available even after getting onboard successfully, as you may need them to exit your arrival station.

P: Good to know. Thank you!

S: That's all right.

Word Tips

automatic	[ˌɔːtəˈmætɪk]	*adj.* 自动的	manually	[ˈmænjʊəli]	*adv.* 人工地

Task 3 Situational practice

Situation 1: Suppose you are a staff member at the boarding gate. A foreign passenger wants to ask you some questions, such as checking and boarding time. Make a conversation with your partner and try to practice it. You can refer to the following picture.

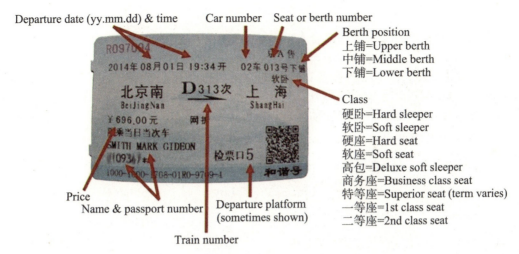

Situation 2: Suppose you are a staff member at the boarding gate. A passenger doesn't know how to check the ticket and need to ask the station staff to get some useful information. Make a conversation with your partner and practice it. You can refer to the picture.

Task 4　Additional practice: phonetics (Plosives)

1. Pronunciation methods

[p] 和 [b]

发[p]音的常见字母与字母组合有p、pp。

发[b]音的常见字母与字母组合有b、bb。

发音方法：[p] 和 [b] 的发音口形相同，双唇爆破辅音。发音时双唇紧闭，憋住气，然后突然分开，气流冲出口腔，发出爆破音。[p]是清辅音，声带不振动；[b]是浊辅音，声带振动。

[t] 和 [d]

发[t]音的常见字母与字母组合有t、tt。

发[d]音的常见字母与字母组合有d、dd。

发音方法：[t] 和 [d] 的发音口形相同，舌齿爆破辅音。发音时舌尖抵上齿龈，憋住气，然后突然分开，使气流冲出口腔，发出爆破音。[t]是清辅音，声带不振动；[d]是浊辅音，声带振动。

[k] 和 [g]

发[k]音的常见字母与字母组合有 k、c、ck。

发[g]音的常见字母与字母组合有 g、gg、gu。

发音方法：[k] 和 [g] 的发音口形相同，舌后软腭爆破辅音。发音时舌后部隆起紧贴软腭，憋住气，然后突然分开，气流送出口腔，形成爆破音。[k]是清辅音，声带不振动；[g]是浊辅音，声带振动。

2. Read and practice

[p]	pepper	upon	piano	pet	apple	happy
[b]	behind	book	bird	boy	rubber	rabbit
[t]	tunnel	table	taxi	tea	matter	butter
[d]	board	duck	desk	dog	bed	opened
[k]	check	cake	cook	milk	clock	sock
[g]	goose	glass	glove	bag	girl	egg

7 Steps to Take a Train in China

Here is a quick guide on how to take trains in China.

Step 1: Arrive at the railway station 1-1.5 hours in advance.

Always make sure that you have some extra time before the departure. Generally, it is recommended to arrive at the station 1 to 1.5 hours before the scheduled departure time.

Step 2: Pass ID-ticket check and security check at the station entrance.

Upon arriving at the station, follow the passenger flow or direction boards to find the entrance and wait in line to get inside. Your ID certificate used for ticket booking will be checked at the entrance. Overseas passengers should use the manual check channel. You will also need to go through security check before going inside.

Step 3: Find the right waiting room and wait for boarding.

In the entrance hall behind the security check there is a large LED screen showing train numbers and corresponding waiting rooms. After finding the waiting room, wait in the specific area closest to the boarding gate of your train.

Step 4: Check in at the right boarding gate.

In most cases, check-in starts 30 minutes before departure and ends 5 minutes before departure in an originating station. If it is an intermediate station, there is only 10-15 minutes for check-in. Your ID certificate used for ticket booking will be checked again at the boarding gate. Also, overseas passengers need to use the manual check channel.

Step 5: Go to the platform for boarding.

After passing the boarding gate, follow the flow of people or the instruction on the LED boards to your platform. After locating the train, find your carriage.

Step 6: Settle the luggage and sit down to enjoy the trip.

After boarding, find your seat. Put your luggage safely on the luggage rack, under your seat or inside the closet between two carriages. Sit down and wait for the departure.

Step 7: Upon arrival, get off and find the way out.

Follow the bilingual direction boards to find exit to leave the station. You need to show your ID certificate again at the manual channel at the exit to leave.

Words and Expressions

departure	[dɪˈpɑːtʃə(r)]	n.	出发	certificate	[səˈtɪfɪkət]	n.	证件
scheduled	[ˈʃedjuːld]	adj.	预定的	corresponding	[ˌkɒrəˈspɒndɪŋ]	adj.	相应的
specific	[spəˈsɪfɪk]	adj.	特定的	originating	[əˈrɪdʒɪneɪtɪŋ]	adj.	起始的
carriage	[ˈkærɪdʒ]	n.	车厢	intermediate	[ˌɪntəˈmiːdiət]	adj.	中间的
rack	[ræk]	n.	架子	bilingual	[ˌbaɪˈlɪŋgwəl]	adj.	双语的
recommend	[ˌrekəˈmend]	v.	推荐				

Task 1 Choose the best answer.

1. Please don't go away and _____ to board _____.
   A. remember; on time   B. keep; in mind   C. care; on time
2. Wuhan station is a _____, boarding starts 30 minutes before train departure.
   A. terminal station   B. intermediate station   C. starting station
3. There are only three minutes before the train departs, _____ has been stopped.
   A. ticket checking   B. safety inspection   C. schedule
4. This is the _____. All the passengers, please get off the train.
   A. starting station   B. intermediate station   C. terminal station
5. The followings are shown on the ticket except _____.
   A. Wechat number   B. boarding gate   C. carriage number

Task 2 Translate the following sentences into Chinese.

1. Always make sure that you have some extra time before the departure.
_____

2. Your ID certificate used for ticket booking will be checked at the entrance.
_____

3. In the entrance hall behind the security check there is a large LED screen showing train numbers and corresponding waiting rooms.
_____

4. Settle the luggage and sit down to enjoy the trip.
_____

5. Follow the bilingual direction boards to find exit to leave the station.
_____

Task 3 Fill in the blanks according to the Chinese meanings.

An Announcement

Ladies and gentlemen, your attention, please. _____(广州局集团有限公司) regrets to _____(通知) that the train G6001 from Changsha South Railway Station to _____(深圳北站) has been delayed for twenty minutes due to technical reasons. We _____(道歉) for any inconvenience it might cause.

...15 minutes later...

Ladies and gentlemen, your attention, please. Train G6001 from Changsha South Railway Station to _____(深圳北站) has arrived. The train is now at _____(2站台) and will leave at 15:25. Please get your tickets and belongings and check in at _____(检票口) No. 8. Thank you for your patience.

Group Work

Task 1 Discuss in groups and complete the table.

The main sources of income for railway companies are ticket sales for passenger transport and shipment fees for cargo. Discounts and monthly passes are sometimes available for frequent travelers. Freight service is charged per containers slot or for a whole train. Sometimes, the freight customers own cars and only buy the haulage. For passenger transportation, advertisement income is significant too. Some local governments may subsidize rail operation, since rail transport has fewer externalities than other public transits.

Group members:
_____

Question	Answer
1. What are the main sources of income for railway companies?	
2. Who can have discounts and monthly passes?	
3. How is freight service charged by train companies?	
4. Why some local governments subsidize railway operations?	
5. What is the main idea of this short passenger?	

Task 2 Translate the following sentences into Chinese one after another within each group.

1. Please wait here, and listen to our broadcasting.
2. Train departure information is on the screens over there.
3. Check-in starts 15 minutes before train's departure time.
4. Train G6002 is now boarding at Gates 5 and 6, please.

5. The train is checking in now. Please be quick.
6. Show me your ticket, please.
7. Please queue up in order.
8. Please take you luggage, have you tickets ready, and line up for boarding.
9. Please use auto gate correctly to check in faster.
10. Check-in will be stopped 3 minutes before train's departure time.
11. Your ticket is overdue. Please buy another one.
12. You missed your train, please change your ticket at the ticket office.

Knowledge Stock

1. Ticket checking mode of High-speed Railway

Usually there are two ways to check in at the railway station—automatic ticket checking and manual ticket checking.

(1) If you hold a blue ticket, you can enter the station through the Automatic Gate Machine. Usually on the right side of the gate, there is a ticket checking device with the words "magnetic ticket entrance". To enter the gate, you need to insert the blue ticket into the slot with the ticket information upward. The gate will open automatically if tickets are valid. In most train stations, passengers can also get through the gate using their ID cards that are used for booking without printing their tickets in advance.

(2) The red ticket holders need to enter the stations through red ticket gates and have their tickets checked manually by station staff. The station staff will validate the tickets by punching a hole on them with ticket clippers.

2. Three conditions for using the second-generation ID card to take the train

Passengers who buy High-speed Railway tickets online do not need to go to the ticket window or automatic ticket vending machine to print their paper tickets. They can put the second-generation ID card on the ID card reader at the automatic ticket gates, and the gate will automatically open for release and enter once the ID cards are validated successfully.

Three conditions are required to use the second-generation ID card to take a train.

(1) Passengers must purchase High-speed Railway tickets online using second-generation ID cards.

(2) Passengers must activate the second-generation ID card ticket checking function when getting on and off the station.

(3) Passengers must not print paper tickets. The electronic ticket function of the ID card will be disable automatically if a paper ticket is printed instead.

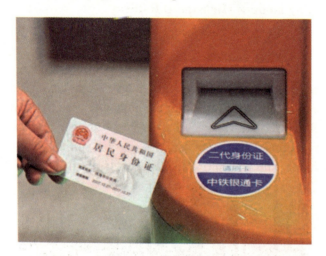

Unit 7 Platform Service

Goals

Understand the facilities and services at the platform;
Learn how to offer help for passengers at platform;
Master the words and expressions about platform service;
Learn about recognizing the colorful marks on the ground of platform.

Warming-up

Task 1 Match the expressions with the pictures.

| Waiting to board | Inbound trains | Station tracks |
| Coach marks | Safety yellow line | Station name sign |

1._____

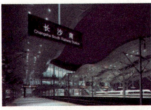

2._____

3._____

4._____

5._____

6._____

63

Task 2 Answer the questions.

1. Can you find out the Chinese equivalents of the phrases in Task 1?
2. What do you know about the landmarks fixed on the platform floor in different colors?

Try to listen

The High-speed Railway broadcasting

Task 1 Listen carefully and fill in the blanks with what you hear.

Dear passengers, attention please. Train G101 from Beijing to Shanghai is now arriving at _____ 2. When the train stops, please make _____ for the passengers to get off first, stay behind the _____ line. The train will _____ at _____. Please get ready to board the train with all your belongings. Thank you for your attention.

Task 2 Read the paragraph in Task 1 loudly and try to recite it.

Conversations

Task 1 Retell the conversations below and imitate the pronunciation and intonation after listening to the recordings.

C 1 Help passengers to find the right coach (帮助乘客找到所在的车厢)

P=Passenger   S=Station staff

S: All passengers, attention please. The train is coming. Please wait behind the safety line.
P: Excuse me, my seat is in the Coach No. 6. Where should I wait?
S: No. 6? Oh, you are going the wrong direction. Go that way, please. The purple signs on the ground will lead you there.
P: Thank you very much. You are a warm-hearted man.
S: I am flattered. Wish you a great journey.

Word Tips

purple	['pɜːpl]	adj.	紫色的	flatter	['flætə(r)]	v.	奉承，使高兴

C 2 Respond to passenger's inquiry (回答乘客的问询)

S: Good afternoon, sir. Welcome to train G52.
P: Good afternoon. Which car is this?
S: This is car No. 2, Sir. Which car are you looking for?
P: I am looking for car No. 8. Here is my ticket.
S: Yes. Your seat is in car No. 8 and it is a window seat. Car No. 8 is the last one. Walk straight

ahead and you will see it.

P: Thanks a lot.

S: You are welcome. Enjoy your trip.

Task 2 Read and role-play the conversations in pairs.

C 1

A: Excuse me, Madam. For your safety, please stand behind the yellow line.

B: Ok, thank you for your kind reminding.

A: It's my duty. Thank you for your cooperation.

B: By the way, can you tell me how long the train will stay at this platform before departure?

A: It will be a few minutes. The train is on time. Is there anything I can help?

B: I am seeing my daughter off. She has large luggage with her. I want to help her to carry her luggage to the train.

A: I see. This is the departure station. You will have enough time for this. There will 10 minutes boarding time before departure.

B: Thanks a lot.

A: My pleasure.

C 2

A: How may I help you?

B: I am afraid I have dislocated my left arm.

A: Don't worry. We can broadcast for doctors and nurses.

B: I can't lift my left arm at all.

A: Don't be nervous. You will be fine.

B: Ouch, my arm.

A: Calm down. We will help you.

B: Thank you.

C 3

A: Excuse me, my iPad dropped into the platform gap. Can you help me to pick it up?

B: Sorry lady, the train is departing. It is very dangerous to pick it up now. I will get the station staff to pick it up after the train leaves.

A: But I am taking this train.

B: Don't worry. You can change your ticket within 2 hours after departure. You can take the train if you are in a hurry, and we can give the phone to the next train. Your phone will be handed over to your destination by the next train.

A: When is the next train to Hangzhou?

B: It's about 30 minutes.

A: Well, I think I would change my ticket.

C 4

S: Madam, you look very tired. Let me help you with your luggage?

P: Oh, thank you for helping me with the luggage. You are so kind.

S: Where are you going?

P: I want to transfer to the train to Wuhan. Should I get out of the station first?

S: Not necessary. With the ticket, you can directly take the barrier-free elevator over there to the waiting hall then find the boarding gate for the train.
P: Could you lead me to the elevator, please?
S: Sure. Let's go.
P: Thank you so much.
S: You are welcome.

C 5

P: Excuse me. Is this Changsha South station?
S: Yes, we are at the Changsha South Railway Station. Please watch out your steps and pay attention to the gap between the train and the platform while alighting the train.
P: Oh, thank you. I am going to Wuyi Square. Do you know how I can get there?
S: Sure, it's very easy. You can take Metro Line 2 and get off at Wuyi Square Station.
P: Thank you! Could you tell me where the subway is?
S: It's just inside the station. You can transfer to the metro at the first floor.
P: Thank you very much.
S: Sure. See you.
P: See you.

Word Tips

transfer	[træns'fɜː(r)]	n. v.	换乘	alight	[ə'laɪt]	v.	下火车
gap	[gæp]	n.	缝隙	square	[skweə(r)]	n.	广场

Task 3　Situational practice

Situation 1: Suppose you are a staff member on the platform. You tell passengers how to stand in line and pay attention to safety. Make a conversation with your partner and try to practice it. You can refer to the following picture.

Situation 2: Suppose you are a staff member on the platform. A female passenger is carrying a child in her arm and pulling a large piece of luggage. You offer help to her. Make a conversation with your partner and try to practice it. You can refer to the following picture.

Task 4　Additional practice: phonetics (Fricatives)

1. Pronunciation methods

[f] 和 [v]

发[f]音的常见字母与字母组合有f、ph、ff、gh。

发[v]音的常见字母有v。

发音方法：[f] 和 [v] 的发音口形相同，唇齿摩擦辅音。发音时上齿轻触下唇，气流由唇齿间通过，形成摩擦音。[f]是清辅音，声带不振动；[v]是浊辅音，声带振动。

[s] 和 [z]

发[s]音的常见字母与字母组合有s、ss、ce、se。

发[z]音的常见字母有s、z。

发音方法：[s] 和 [z] 的发音口形相同，舌齿摩擦辅音。发音时舌端靠近齿龈，气流由舌端齿龈间送出，形成摩擦音。[s]是清辅音，声带不振动；[z]是浊浦音，声带振动。

[ʃ] 和 [ʒ]

发[ʃ]音的常见字母与字母组合有s、ch、sh。

发[ʒ]音的常见字母与字母组合有s、ge。

发音方法：[ʃ] 和 [ʒ] 的发音口形相同，舌端齿龈后部摩擦辅音。发音时舌端靠近齿龈后部，舌身抬起靠近上颚，双唇稍收圆并略突出。气流通过时形成摩擦音。[ʃ]是清辅音，声带不振动；[ʒ]是浊辅音，声带振动。

2. Read and practice

[f]	photo	before	find	follow	platform	phone
[v]	village	have	leave	very	victory	vocabulary
[s]	Saturday	advance	schedule	station	some	security
[z]	size	conversations	always	overseas	passengers	amaze
[ʃ]	share	sure	friendship	she	finish	should
[ʒ]	treasure	usually	pleasure	decision	conclusion	revision

Reading

Tips of Recognizing the Colorful Marks on the Ground of Platform

Nowadays, there are more and more High-speed Railway lines, making it easier for people to travel. When taking the High-speed Railway, many people may notice that on the platform where the high-speed train stops, there are some signs fixed on the platform floor, marked with the car number of this place and other car direction arrows, and they are also divided into yellow, green, blue and purple colors. What are their functions?

According to authoritative sources, these are the land signs designed to help the passengers quickly find the corresponding location of the car.

When most EMUs are numbered as singular, car No.1 is generally in the front direction, car No. 8/16 are in the rear direction, and vice versa, when EMUs are numbered as even. The former one is called as positive marshalling, while the latter one is reverse marshalling.

Generally speaking, there are several colors on the platform: blue stands for long 16-car positive marshalling, yellow represents long 16-car reverse marshalling, green represents 8-car positive marshalling, and purple represents 8-car reverse marshalling. Because there are many trains in and out of the station every day, one platform will pick up and send trains in different directions, so the order of carriages will be different naturally due to different directions.

At the same time, during the peak period of passenger flow, there are more passengers going to some directions. The railway department will reconnect multiple units (16 cars), so that there are both 8 and 16 trains. Therefore, the "landmark" position on the platform has changed.

Words and Expressions

function	[dɪˈpɑːtʃə(r)]	n.	功能	represent	[ˌreprɪˈzent]	n.	代表
vice versa	[ˌvaɪs ˈvɜːsə]	adv.	反之亦然	location	[ləʊˈkeɪʃn]	n.	位置
singular	[ˈsɪŋɡjələ(r)]	n.	单数	marshalling	[ˈmɑːʃəlɪŋ]	v.	编组
authoritative	[ɔːˈθɒrətətɪv]	adj.	权威的				

Task 1 Choose the best answer.

1. What is not included in the signs fixed on the platform floor _____.
   A. car number   B. car direction arrows   C. seat number

2. Usually when the EMU is named as singular, car No. 1 is located at the _____ direction.
   A. rear   B. front   C. tail

3. If the EMU is numbered as G502, it is often _____ marshalling.
   A. reverse   B. positive   C. random

4. The blue color on the platform ground stands for _____.
   A. 8-car reverse marshalling
   B. long 16-car positive marshalling
   C. long 16-car reverse marshalling
5. The purple color on the platform ground stands for _____.
   A. long 16-car positive marshalling
   B. 8-car reverse marshalling
   C. 8-car positive marshalling

Task 2   Translate the following sentences into Chinese.

1. Nowadays, there are more and more High-speed Railway lines, making it easier for people to travel.
   _____

2. There are some signs fixed on the platform floor, marked with the car number of this place and other car direction arrows.
   _____

3. According to authoritative sources, these are the land signs designed to help the passengers quickly find the corresponding location of the car.
   _____

4. When most EMUs are numbered as singular, car No. 1 is generally in the front direction.
   _____

5. Blue stands for long 16-car positive marshalling, yellow represents long 16-car reverse marshalling.
   _____

Task 3   Fill in the blanks according to the Chinese meanings.

Boarding Platforms

After your ticket has been checked, follow the instruction on the LED screen or everyone else and go through your _____(检票口) to your platform. In some circumstances, you may need to take some stairs, or take the _____(直梯) or _____(自动扶梯) to get to your platform.

There may be trains on both side of a platform. Look for the train number and board the one that you are taking. The _____(检票员) standing by the doors will request a ticket check but not an ID check. Double-check with the inspector if you are not sure if it's the right train. The high-speed train usually stops right below the _____(登车口).

Group Work

Task 1   Discuss in groups and complete the table.

Railway tracks are laid upon land owned or leased by the railway company. Owing to the desirability of maintaining modest grades, rails will often be laid in circuitous routes in hilly or mountainous terrain. Route length and grade requirements can be reduced by the use of alternative cuttings, bridges and tunnels, all of which can greatly increase the capital expenditures required to develop a railway track, while significantly reducing operating costs and allowing higher speeds on longer radius curves. In densely urbanized areas, railways are sometimes laid in tunnels to minimize the effects on existing properties.

Group members:

Question	Answer
1. What is the main idea of this short passage?	
2. Whether all the railway tracks are laid upon land owned by the railway company?	
3. Why are rails often laid in circuitous routes in hilly or mountainous terrain?	
4. How to reduce operating costs?	
5. Why are railways sometimes laid in tunnels in densely urbanized areas?	

Task 2   **Translate the following sentences into Chinese one after another within each group.**

1. For your safety, please stay behind the yellow line.
2. Please look after your children and mind the gap between the train and the platform.
3. Your luggage looks heavy. Let me help you with it.
4. The train G6001 will stay at the platform for five minutes before departure.
5. Please take your luggage and get ready for boarding.
6. The train is at the Platform 2, please board quickly.
7. Is this the right platform for the train to Beijingxi?
8. A railway platform is a section of pathway, alongside rail tracks at a railway station, where passengers may board or alight from trains.
9. Platform service mainly deals with passengers' boarding and alighting.
10. As a passenger clerk at platform, you need ensure that all passengers can get on and off the train safely and smoothly.
11. Once you have stepped off the train and are behind the safety line, do not cross it back once again. Please proceed to the station exits.
12. To prevent identity theft, please keep your ticket yourself.

Knowledge Stock

1. List of graphic symbols

No.	Graphic symbols	Chinese & English meaning	Instructions
1		售票处 Tickets	表示出售火车票的场所
2		补票处 Pay upon arrival	表示查、补火车票的场所
3		检票口 Check-in	表示铁路火车站检票的位置
4		信息服务 Information service	表示提供信息服务的场所
5		男卫生间 Men	表示男性卫生间
6		女卫生间 Women	表示女性卫生间

71

No.	Graphic symbols	Chinese & English meaning	Instructions
7		卫生间 Restrooms	表示男女卫生间内分别设有无障碍设施
8		卫生间 Restrooms	表示卫生间内设有单独的无障碍卫生间
9		行李托运、提取 Baggage check-in and claim	表示办理行李托运和提取的位置
10		行包房 Baggage	表示提供行李包裹等服务的场所
11		饮用水 Drinking water	表示提供可饮用水的场所或位置
12		VIP候车室 VIP waiting room	表示提供 VIP 服务的候车场所
13		客运值班室 Passenger transport office	表示铁路客运人员执勤或办公的场所
14		公安值班室 Security	表示安全保卫人员执勤或办公的场所

No.	Graphic symbols	Chinese & English meaning	Instructions
15		便捷换乘 Transfer	表示铁路客运车站内引导旅客便捷换乘的标识
16		小心站台间隙 Caution gap	表示站台边缘的警示标识
17		旅客止步 Staff only	表示该处不允许旅客进入、通行或穿越
18		禁止通行 No thoroughfare	表示该处禁止进入、通行或穿越

2. Platform naming

When there are multiple platforms, platform number identification shall be set. The platform number starts from the basic platform. The basic platform is numbered as platform 1, and the number of other platforms is arranged from small to large according to the distance from the basic platform. If there are two basic platforms, the platform on one side of the main station room or the main source of passenger flow is defined as platform 1.

Sketch map:

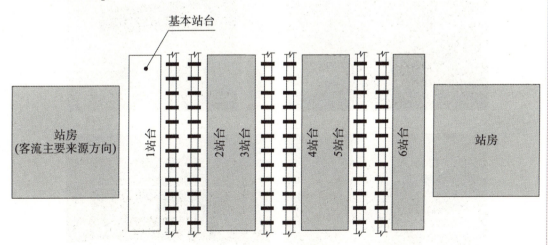

Unit 8 Arrival

Goals

Be familiar with the issues of arrival services;
Grasp the useful expressions of arrival services;
Know how to remind passengers to get off the train;
Know how to help passengers exit.

Warming-up

Try to think

Task 1 Match the words and expressions with the pictures.

Railway station exit　　　　Transfer
Pay upon arrival　　　　　　Direction signboard

1._____ 2._____

3._____ 4._____

Task 2   What do the following signs stand for? Write the English name for each of them.

    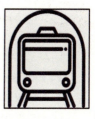

1._____   2._____   3._____   4._____   5._____

Try to listen

The High-speed Railway broadcasting

Task 1   Listen carefully and fill in the blanks with what you hear.

Ladies and gentlemen, we are approaching _____ Station at _____ and stop for 3 minutes. As the train will stop for only a few minutes, please do not get off the train if it isn't your destination. For passengers who need to offboard, please check your luggage and be ready to get off the train. The door will open on the _____ side. Please exit from the front door in each carriage and let passengers alight first before boarding the train. The platform is slippery due to the snow. Please mind your _____ while getting off the train. Passengers who hold paper tickets and need to change trains please follow the _____ sign and go back to the station hall. The nearest transfer passage is next to coach 10.

Task 2   Read the paragraph in Task 1 loudly and try to recite it.

Task 1   Retell the conversations below and imitate the pronunciation and intonation, after listening to the recordings.

C 1   Serve passengers transfer between different vehicles (换乘交通工具)

P=Passenger   S=Station staff

P: Excuse me, how can I get to Chunxi Road from Chengdu East Railway Station?
S: You can get a taxi here. It will take about 25 minutes to the Chunxi Road.
P: How about subway?
S: You can take Metro Line 2. There are about 6 stops before Chunxi Road. It will take about 15 minutes. Another option is taking a bus, but it takes much more time.
P: How long will it take by bus?
S: About 1 hour.

P: Yes. It's too long! I will take the subway. Is there a subway station nearby?

S: Yes. After getting out of the main hall, you can take the escalator to one level down. The Metro Line 2 is on your left.

P: Thank you.

C 2　Transfer to another train (便携换乘)

P: Excuse me, I am looking for my connecting train. Can you please help me with it?

S: Show me your ticket, please.

P: Here you are.

S: Changsha, ok. It is also in this station but at a different platform.

P: How can I get there?

S: Follow the transfer signs and LED screen. You will find the waiting room for your connecting train.

P: Thank you.

S: You are welcome.

Task 2　Read and role-play the conversations in pairs.

C 1

S: Excuse me. I can't find my grandma.

P: Don't worry. We will help you. What is her name and how does she look like?

S: Her name is Nancy Li. She is seventy years old and has a senile dementia.

P: When and where did this happen?

S: About ten minutes ago, in the dining car. We were having lunch before I went to the restroom. However, when I came back, she was gone!

P: Any other information that can help people to identify her? For example, what she is wearing?

S: She is wearing a pink dress and carrying a silver handbag. Also, she has grey curly hair.

P: That is helpful. I will first call her to return to the dining car. And then ask any people who saw her contact the conductor.

S: Thank you.

C 2

S: Good afternoon, what can I do for you?

P: My luggage was lost on the train yesterday.

S: Which train did you choose?

P: G212 train from Dalian to Harbin.

S: At what time did you board the train?

P: I got on the train in the morning at 10 o'clock.

S: What is your luggage like?

P: It was a tourist bag. Light Red in color.

S: Show me your ID proof and ticket please.

P: Sure, here you are.

S: As soon as we get any update, we will get in touch with you. Just give us 24 hours.

P: Thank you, sir. I will be waiting anxiously for your call.

C 3

S: Excuse me, how can I get to Rujia Hotel near the railway station?

P: You can walk there. It takes only about 15 minutes by walking from the railway station. You can enjoy the city view on your way too!

S: Great! Thank you. I will just walk. How can I get there?

P: After you get out of the station, turn left and walk straight for about 15 minutes until you see a big supermarket. The hotel is right opposite to the supermarket. You can't miss it.

S: Thanks again!

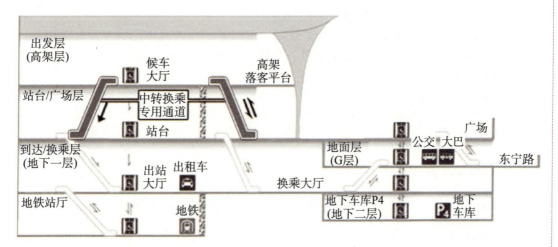

Task 3　Situational practice

Situation 1: Suppose you are a station staff member in the sleeping car. A passenger lost a wallet at the railway station, what will you do? How can you get her things back? You offer help to her. Make a conversation with your partner and try to practice it. You can refer to the following information.

- Date item was lost: June 16, 2020.
- Where the item was lost: Harbin Railway station.
- A thorough description of the wallet: The wallet is brown with ID card and several money in it.
- Phone number:12345678900.

Situation 2: Suppose you are the conductor on the train. Before the train arrives at a transfer station, a foreign passenger need to get off the train. You offer help to her. Use the useful words and expressions that you have learned to make a conversation with your partner and try to practice it. You can refer to the following expressions.

- Please remind me to prepare to get off at this station 10 minutes before arrival.
- Please take all your belongings and get off the train in order.
- Please mind the gap between the train and the platform.
- Please exit from the rear door in the direction of travel.
- Miss one's stop.
- Arrive on time/ half an hour behind schedule.

Task 4   Additional practice: phonetics (Fricatives)

1. Pronunciation methods

[θ] 和 [ð]

[θ]和[ð]是字母组合th的发音。

发音方法：[θ] 和 [ð] 的发音口形相同，舌齿摩擦辅音。发音时舌尖轻触上齿背，气流由舌齿间送出，形成摩擦音。[θ]是清辅音，声带不振动；[ð]是浊辅音，声带振动。

[h]

发[h]音的常见字母与字母组合有h、wh。

发音方法：声门摩擦辅音。发音时气流送出口腔，在通过声门时发出轻微摩擦；口形随其后的元音而变化。[h]是清辅音，声带不振动。

[r]

发[r]音的常见字母与字母组合有r、rr、wr。

发音方法：舌尖齿龈(后部)摩擦辅音。发音时舌尖卷起，靠近上齿龈后部；舌两侧稍收拢，双唇略突出；气流通过舌尖和齿龈形成轻微摩擦。[r]是浊辅音，声带振动。

2. Read and practice

[θ]	mouth	thank	think	through	thumb	something
[ð]	weather	they	theme	those	there	than
[h]	heart	hand	hurry	help	high	hope
[r]	write	reason	correct	train	breakthrough	relevant

Disembarking from High-speed Trains

　　Station announcements usually made at least 10 minutes before each stop, to give passengers time to prepare to leave the train. Bilingual announcements are available on most high-speed trains. LED displays located above the front door in each carriage on high-speed trains will keep passengers informed of the real-time speed and arrival stations in both Chinese and English.

　　Railway attendants will remind passengers to pack their luggage and personal belongings in advance. In case that passengers left any items on the train, they can report their losses at Lost and Found. When trains arrive at the station, passengers will be asked get off the train in order.

　　On the platform, there are bilingual direction signboards. Passengers can follow the crowd and the overhead instruction sign of "Exit (出站口)" to the exit, Taxi stand, metro station, bus station, etc. In some stations, there are Red Cap porters who can help passengers with their bulky luggage.

　　At the exit, passengers need to place or insert their tickets or personal ID to the automatic ticket checking machine to leave the station. It is recommended that transfer passengers get their tickets all at once at the first departure station. In this way, they don't need to get out of the station and re-enter if the connecting train is at the same station.

Words and Expressions

announcement	[əˈnaʊnsmənt]	n.	通告	bulky　[ˈbʌlki]	adj. 笨重的
display	[dɪˈspleɪ]	v.	显示	keep...informed of	被通知……
real-time	[ˌriːəlˈtaɪm]	adj.	实时的	in case	以防；万一
attendant	[əˈtendənt]	n.	服务员	Lost and Found	失物招领
item	[ˈaɪtəm]	n.	物品	in order	井然有序
signboard	[ˈsaɪnbɔːd]	n.	告示牌	Taxi stand	出租车站
overhead	[ˌəʊvəˈhed]	adv.	在头上方	bilingual direction signboard	双语方向指示牌

Task 1　Read the text and decide whether the following statements are **T** (true) or **F** (false).

　　(　　) 1. Passengers will be reminded to check their luggage and get ready to get off when the train arrives at the station.

　　(　　) 2. Following bilingual direction signboards, passengers could find the exit in all stations.

　　(　　) 3. If passengers take bulky belongings, Red Cap Luggage Service is available for them in some large stations.

　　(　　) 4. Passengers' tickets are need to be checked at the exit.

(　　) 5. There is no need for transfer passengers with the previous ticket to exit and re-enter at the same transfer stations.

Task 2　Translate the following sentences into Chinese.

1. Station announcements usually made at least 10 minutes before each stop, to give passengers time to prepare to leave the train.
_____

2. In case that passengers left any items on the train, they can report their losses at Lost and Found.
_____

3. Passengers can follow the crowd and the overhead instruction sign of "Exit (出站口)" to the exit, Taxi stand, metro station, bus station, etc.
_____

4. In some stations, there are Red Cap porters who can help passengers with their bulky luggage.
_____

5. It is recommended that transfer passengers get their tickets all at once at the first departure station.
_____

Task 3　Fill in the blanks according to the Chinese meaning.

City Transportation From a Train Station

You can find transportation _____ (标志) for taxi, bus and subway easily around the station. Usually the _____ (运行) time of buses and subway is from 5:00 to 23:00. Taxies are available 24 hours a day. But in large cities such as Beijing, Shanghai, Guangzhou and Xi'an, you might need to wait in long _____ (队伍) for taxis, especially during rush hour _____ (高峰期). Buses and subways are always _____ (拥挤).

Group Work

Task 1　Look at the chart and discuss in groups the details about the following services. Make a report about the introduction of these services in English within each group.

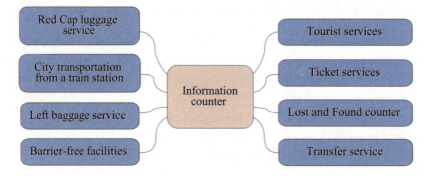

Task 2 Match the English in column A with their corresponding Chinese in column B.

A	B
Lost and Found counter	信息咨询处
Red Cap luggage service	游客服务中心
Left baggage service	便捷换乘
Barrier-free facilities	无障碍服务
City transportation	城市交通
Information counters	行李存放处
Transfer service	小红帽行李服务
Tourist service	失物招领处

Knowledge Stock

1. Get off the high-speed trains step by step

Getting off a high-speed train is much easier than getting on it!

Watch your stop   Get off the train   Ticket check for exit   Follow the signs and exit the station

(1) Watch your stop.

If your destination is not the terminus of the train, you need to listen to the stop announcements and pay attention to stop information on the LED screen, both in English and Chinese, carefully. Station announcements usually come at least 10 minutes before each stop to give travelers time to prepare for collecting their baggage off the racks to get off the train. If you get confused, it is strongly advised that you show your tickets to a member of the train staff or just a passenger next to you and ask her/him to remind you to get off. You could write or type a word like: "到这个车站请提醒我下车，谢谢！(which means that please remind me to get off the train while arriving at this stop, thank you!)"

(2) Get off your train.

Please remember to take your whole luggage and all belongs with you when embark the high-speed train. In a stop at a large city like Beijing, Shanghai, Chengdu, Xi'an, etc. or the terminus stop, you could take your time to avoid the crowd in the aisle and train exit. However, it has usually only 2-3 minutes' stop in a not very big train station. If so, please get off the train with all your baggage as quick and safe as possible. If you feel it a little hurry, you are suggested take your luggage to wait at the train door as it gives the announcement.

Once you land on the platform, you will see clear signs above head showing you the way out. To make it simpler, you can just follow the crowd and then successfully get to the correct exit for ticket checking again.

(3) Check your train ticket at the gate machine.

Before you walk out of the train station, you are required to check your ticket again for exit. Just do like you check your ticket before getting on a train, insert your ticket into the slot of the machine and take it after is coming out. Please choose a machine with green light at the slot. Machines with slot with red light are not available temporarily. If your ticket cannot go through the checking machine successfully, please go through the manual checking passage.

(4) Ground transportation.

Subways, taxis, buses or coaches are all available in some big cities. And in some not very prosperous destinations, they also have buses and taxis for your easy transfer to the downtown and the scenic areas. No matter where you are in the station, the logical and conspicuous signs and arrows will tell you where to take a taxi, subway, bus, airport shuttle bus, or distance coaches and way to different exits of the station.

2. What should foreign passengers prepare for transferring to another train?

(1) Tickets.

They need at least two tickets to finish the whole journey if they can't go to their destination directly, and it is recommended that they collect their tickets all at once at their departure stations to save time.

(2) Passport.

They are required to show their passports when entering into a Chinese railway station, and you might also need to show it during the transfer.

3. "Zero transfer, seamless" in HSR comprehensive transportation hub

Section III
Train Service

Unit 9 Boarding Service

Goals

Master the useful expressions about welcoming passengers aboard;
Learn to help passengers find his/her seat after he/she get on the train;
Be able to help passengers arrange their baggage;
Learn about the differences between Normal Train and High-speed Train.

Warming-up

Task 1 Match the words and expressions with the pictures.

Vibrant Express	T-Express	Rejuvenation
Harmony	Z-Non-Stop Express	K-Fast

1._____

2._____

3._____

4._____

5._____

6._____

Task 2   What should a train attendant do when passengers get aboard the train?

Try to listen

The High-speed Railway broadcasting

Task 1   Listen carefully and fill in the blanks with what you hear.

Dear passengers, welcome _____ the train. It's my pleasure to extend our best regards to you on behalf of all the crew members. Please confirm your train _____ and destination. Please be _____ according to the seat number on your ticket. Your belongings should be placed safely on the _____ racks or in the luggage space at the end of the coach. Please _____ to the Train Service Guide or consult the crew members if you want to know more about the coach facilities.

Task 2   Read the paragraph in Task 1 loudly and try to recite it.

Task 1   Retell the conversations below and imitate the pronunciation and intonation after listening to the recordings.

C 1   **Help passengers find seats** (寻找座位)

C=Train crew member   P=Passenger

P: Excuse me, madam. Where is my seat? I can't find it.
C: Could you show me your ticket, please?
P: Here you are.
C: Oh, your seat number is 50, it is on the 9th row from the other end. The seat is on your left. Take this way and you won't miss it.
P: Much appreciated.
C: My pleasure. Mind your steps.

Word Tips

| miss | [mɪs] | v. | 错过 | appreciate | [əˈpriːʃieɪt] | v. | 感谢 |
| pleasure | [ˈpleʒə(r)] | n. | 荣幸 | mind | [maɪnd] | v. | 留神；当心 |

C 2 Remind passengers to get on board (提醒旅客上车)

P: Excuse me, when does the train leave?

C: The train is leaving at nine to Beijing. You can listen to the broadcasting for boarding information.

P: I see. How much time is left till 9?

C: Three minutes. Please hurry up if you take this train.

Task 2 Read and role-play the conversations in pairs.

C=Train crew member   P=Passenger

C 1

P: Excuse me, I have bad eyesight. Could you please help me to check what my train number is?

C: Of course, let me see. Your train is G31, it's on the other side of the platform.

P: Thanks. Could you also tell me my seat number?

C: Sure. Your seat is No. 1. It's a VIP seat. Let me show you. This way, please.

C 2

C: (To another passenger) Excuse me, sir. Is this your suitcase?

P: Yes, it's mine. What's wrong with it?

C: It's too large for overhead rack. It could slip off the rack anytime. That's a safety hazard. Please take it down and put it under your seat.

P: I see. Thank you for the reminding. I will take it off.

C: Don't mention it. Come on, let me give you a hand.

C 3

C: Good morning. Welcome aboard. This way, please.

P: Thank you. Madam, can you guide me to my seat?

C: Certainly. May I see your ticket, please?

P: Sure. Here it is.

C: Your seat is in the middle of the cabin on the left.

P: Got it. By the way, I have too much luggage, could you help me to bring them to my seat? I am afraid I can't manage them.

C: My pleasure. Go along with me, please. Your seat is here.
P: Oh, thank you.
C: Your luggage is here. Please take care of them.
P: It's very nice of you. Thank you very much.
C: Sure.

Task 3　Situational practice

Situation 1: Suppose you are an attendant on the train. It's time for you to give a brief speech about welcoming. Try to make up a speech by yourself and practice it in your class.

Situation 2: Suppose you are an attendant on the train. A passenger can't find her berth. You offer help to her. Make a conversation with your partner and practice it. The following is for your reference.

上铺：upper berth　　　中铺：middle berth　　　下铺：lower berth

Task 4　Additional practice: phonetics (Affricates)

1. Pronunciation methods

[tʃ] 和 [dʒ]

发[tʃ]音的常见字母与字母组合有t、ch、tch、ti、ture。

发[dʒ]音的常见字母与字母组合有j、g、(d)ge。

发音方法：[tʃ] 和 [dʒ] 的发音口形相同，舌端齿龈破擦辅音。发音时舌身抬高，舌端抵上齿龈后部，气流通过时发出破擦音。[tʃ]是清辅音，声带不振动；[dʒ]是浊辅音，声带振动。

[tr] 和 [dr]

发[tr]音的常见字母组合有tr。

发[dr]音的常见字母组合有dr。

发音方法：[tr] 和[dr] 的发音口形相同，齿龈后部破擦辅音。发音时双唇收圆略向前突出，舌尖贴齿龈后部，气流冲破阻碍而发出声音。[tr]是清辅音，声带不振动；[dr]是浊辅音，声带振动。

[ts] 和 [dz]

发[ts]音的常见字母组合有ts、tes。

发[dz]音的常见字母组合有ds、des。

发音方法：[ts] 和 [dz] 的发音口形相同，属破擦音，舌端齿龈破擦辅音。舌端先贴住齿龈，堵住气流，然后略下降，气流送出口腔。[ts]是清辅音，声带不振动；[dz]是浊辅音，声带振动。

2. Read and practice

[tʃ]	teach	China	coach	question	culture	match
[dʒ]	bridge	generally	luggage	jacket	adjust	procedure
[tr]	trolley	try	victory	secretary	treat	extra
[dr]	drink	drive	dream	dress	drum	drug
[ts]	sweets	boats	tickets	minutes	respondents	toilets
[dz]	cards	boards	modes	woods	spreads	attendants

Reading

The Main Differences Between Regular Train and High-speed Train

Experiencing high-speed train is the must-do activity in China. Check out the differences between regular trains and high-speed trains and you will get to know "why taking high-speed train instead of regular train".

Huge speed difference: 160 km/h vs. 400 km/h.

The highest speed of regular trains would not exceed 160 km/h (99 mph) while the top speed of bullet train could reach up to 400 km/h like Fuxing trains. That's to say, the speed of a high-speed train is two to three times faster than regular trains. Regular trains stop as many stations as possible while high-speed trains stop at only a few main stations. Your train travel time will be shortened significantly if taking the high-speed train. For example, for travelers who travel from Beijing to Chengdu, the trip takes about 8-10 hours by the high-speed G train and 21-30 hours by the regular K or Z trains. Higher speed and fewer stops make the high-speed train the top choice for many travelers including tourists. Tourists can save more time on traveling and spend more on in-depth sightseeing.

Seat classes & price difference: more comfortable on high-speed train.

Regular trains:

Seat types	Seats	Features
Hard seats	2+3 seats in a row	Crowded, noisy
Hard sleepers	2 upper, 2 middle, 2 lower sleepers	Open compartment, less crowded
Soft sleepers	2 lower berths and 2 upper berths in each cabin	Each compartment is a single cabin with a private door facing the aisle
Standing tickets	No seats	Stand in hard seats carriages uncomfortably

High-speed train:

Seat types	Seats	Features
Second class	2+3 seats in a row	Less crowded, but passenger may talk loudly
First class	2+2 seats in a row	Quiet, comfortable, spacious
Business class	1+1 or 1+2 seats in a row	Highest level of comfort, superior service in the entire journey
Soft sleeper	2 or 4 in a cabin	Equipped only in the overnight D trains, very comfortable

Note: 1. In some circumstance, the hard seat in a regular train is almost 70% cheaper than the second class seat of a high-speed train. And the soft sleeper of a regular train is almost 75% cheaper than the business class seat of a high-speed train.

    2. If you take regular trains, you'd better choose hard sleeper or soft sleeper.

    3. If you take high-speed trains, it is recommended to take first class seats for comfort.

Facilities: basic equipment vs. advanced facilities.

The facilities on regular trains are very basic—luggage rack, dining car, food trolley, air-condition, toilets, washbasin, drinking water, electricity charging sockets, TV, smoking area. No Wi-Fi and internet access on regular trains.

While, travelers can enjoy advanced facilities on a high-speed train—luggage rack, medium and large luggage lockers, electricity charging sockets on your seats, dining car, food trolley, drinking water, sit toilets and squat toilets, baby care room, barrier-free restroom, washbasin, TV screen, newspaper and magazine, blinder, blanket, headset and more. Wi-Fi is available and smoking is not allowed on high-speed train!

Words and Expressions

experiencing	[ɪk'spɪəriənsɪŋ]	v.	体验	circumstance	['sɜːkəmstəns]	n.	环境
tour	[tʊə(r)]	n.	旅游	recommend	[ˌrekə'mend]	v.	建议
exceed	[ɪk'siːd]	v.	超过	rack	[ræk]	n.	架子
shorten	['ʃɔːtn]	v.	缩短	trolley	['trɒli]	n.	手推车
save	[seɪv]	v.	节省	socket	['sɒkɪt]	n.	插座
sightseeing	['saɪtsiːɪŋ]	n.	观光	access	['ækses]	n.	通道
compartment	[kəm'pɑːtmənt]	n.	车厢	blinder	['blaɪndə(r)]	n.	眼罩
spacious	['speɪʃəs]	adj.	宽敞的	available	[ə'veɪləbl]	adj.	可获得的

Task 1   Choose the best answer.

1. Which one below is not the main difference between regular train and high-speed train?
   A. Huge speed difference.   B. Facilities difference.   C. Service difference.
2. The top speed of high-speed trains in China could reach up to _____.
   A. 400 km/h   B. 500 km/h   C. 350 km/h
3. Is Wi-Fi available on high-speed trains?
   A. Not mentioned.   B. Yes, it is.   C. No, it isn't.
4. Is smoking allowed on regular trains?
   A. Not mentioned.   B. Yes, it is.   C. No, it isn't.
5. If you take high-speed trains, it is recommended to take _____ for comfort.
   A. first class seats   B. second class seats   C. soft sleepers

Task 2   Translate the following sentences into Chinese.

1. Check out the differences between regular trains and high-speed trains in China.

_____

2. Higher speed and fewer stops make the high-speed trains the top choice for many travelers including tourists.

_____

3. If you take high-speed trains, it is recommended to take first class seats for comfort.

_____

4. Travelers can enjoy advanced facilities on a high-speed train.
_____

5. Wi-Fi is available and smoking is not allowed on high-speed trains.
_____

Task 3　Fill in the blanks according to the Chinese meanings.

Board and Disembark Guidance

Once you arrived at the entrance door of your _____ (车厢), you can see an attendant standing beside the door. When the train arrived at the last station, the attendant will stand beside the door too. Actually, there will be _____ (引导服务) in the entire trip in a high speed train. When you are _____ (上车), the attendant will _____ (检票) and give you _____ (温馨提示), for example, the gap between the carriage and railway platform. When the train stops at a station, the attendants will check _____ (是否有人在外面吸烟).

Task 1　Traveling by train or by plane? Complete the chart and collect more details in groups about the advantages of traveling by high-speed train. Each group discuss about the most impressive travel experience. Then one of your group members will share the experience to other groups.

Items	By high-speed trains	By plane
Travel expenses		
Travel time		
Travel environment experience		

Task 2　Match the English in column A with their corresponding Chinese in column B.

A	B
Higher speed at 250-400 km/h	亲近孩子
More punctual & reliable	户外景观的独特体验
Safe & comfortable	更便宜
Kids friendly	安全舒适
Cheaper	便利的设施和功能
Unique experience with landscape outside	更准时、可靠
Handy facilities & functions	方便进入市区
Easy access to the city	节省时间
Time saving	静音车厢
Environment friendly	以250~400 km/h的速度行驶
Quiet car	环保

Knowledge Stock

1. Fuxing trains—newest and fastest bullet trains in China

On June 26, 2017, China's Fuxing (rejuvenation, 复兴号) trains made its debut. At 11:05 a.m., the first Fuxing train G123 (CR400AF Model) departed from Beijing South Railway Station to Shanghai. At the same time, G124 (CR400BF Model) ran from Shanghai Hongqiao Railway Station to Beijing. It means that the remarkable Fuxing trains went into operation.

Fuxing Hao(left) and Hexie Hao(right)

The average designed speed of Fuxing trains is about 350 km/h, over 100 km/h faster than Hexie trains. The highest operating speed reaches to 400 km/h, which is also the highest operating speed of China's trains. Beijing-Shanghai Tour is one of the most popular routes in China, which makes Beijing-Shanghai Railway become one of the busiest railways. At present, the travel time of Beijing-Shanghai High-speed Railway has been cut down to about 4 hours from 5 hours before.

Many components of Hexie trains are imported from overseas, but Fuxing trains are entirely designed and manufactured by Chinese. More than 20 Chinese firms have been involved in this project over the past three years. They made a great progress in the history of the high-speed trains. These new trains underpin unique role that High-speed Railway has played in China's economic and social development.

2. Features of Fuxing trains—nicer, larger, safer and faster

Feature	Picture	Introduction
Longer life span	Fuxing Bullet Train	With the especially designed components, Fuxing trains enjoy a longer life span, which reaches as long as 30 years, about 10 years longer than Hexie trains. The existing Hexie trains that have been in service for 10 years, are expected to be replaced by Fuxing trains in the near future
Nicer appearance	China's Newest Fuxing Train	Different from other-typed EMU trains, Fuxing trains have several marginal improvements. The locomotive of Fuxing trains is carefully designed and decorated with red or golden. Because of its shape, the air resistance is reduced by 7.5%-12.3% and the energy consumption in every 100 kilometers is reduced by 17%. Undoubtedly, the operating speed is much higher

Feature	Picture	Introduction
Larger space	Business Class on Fuxing Trains	The inside is much more spacious. The height of the car increases from 3.7-4.05 m. The space between the front seats and rear seats is about 1.02 m in the Second Class seats and 1.16 m in the First Class seats. It is much easier for passengers to stretch to their legs. In comparison, the space between the front and rear seats in Hexie trains is only about 1-1.1 m
Free Wi-Fi	LED Screen for Seat Information	Free Wi-Fi coverage is offered on all Fuxing bullet trains. There is no password required, thus passengers can access internet services using smart phones and laptops while traveling at a speed over 350 km/h
More user-friendly	Automatic Door on Fuxing Trains	While designing Fuxing trains, the Mechanical Engineers always took customer experience into consideration. There are more humanized designs that passengers can find in Fuxing trains. Free Wi-Fi is provided to accommodate travelers' needs. In addition, charger plugs is moved to the back of the front seats from the bottom of the seats to make it more convenient for passengers. There is also an USB connector near the plug. The connections between two cars are equipped with baggage holders for passengers with stand tickets

Unit 10 Carriage Service

Goals

Learn about the service on high-speed trains;
Learn to explain the railway regulations to passengers;
Offer help for passengers with problems on high-speed trains;
Help passengers to use facilities and resources on the train.

Warming-up

Try to think

Task 1 Match the expressions with the pictures.

Cleaning service
Service for special passengers
Food & drink service
Checking & registration service
Board and disembark guidance
Broadcast service

1._____

2._____

3._____

4._____

5._____

6._____

Task 2 What other services can be provided for passengers on the train?

The High-speed Railway broadcasting

Task 1 Listen carefully and fill in the blanks with what you hear.

Ladies and gentlemen, to _____ a tidy and comfortable traveling environment, please take good care of the facilities in the carriage. The _____ table in front of you is for holding books and _____. To avoid injuries, please do not put _____ things or _____ on it.

Task 2 Read the paragraph in Task 1 loudly and recite it.

Task 1 Retell the conversations below and imitate the pronunciation and intonation after listening to the recordings.

C1 Explain the railway regulations to passengers (向旅客解释规章制度)

C=Train crew member   P=Passenger

P: Excuse me. What's the top speed that the train can reach? It is running very fast now.

C: The top speed is 350 km/h. But all the windows are made of decelerating glass, so you won't have the feeling of dizziness.

P: What's the speed of the train now?

C: The current speed is shown on the electronic screen at the end of each car. It is about 280 km/h.

P: I see. That is awesome. Is there a smoking area where can I smoke?

C: I'm afraid not. Smoking is not allowed on the train.

P: But passengers can smoke in a restricted area on a normal train.

C: Yes. But not on a high-speed train. It is a CRH2 train. The smoke detection system are from the Japanese company Kawasaki. They are sensitive enough to detect a tiny amount of smoke. Once the alarm goes off, the train will stop automatically. In that case, the train will be delayed.

P: I see. Thank you for your explanation.

C: You are welcome.

Word Tips

| decelerate | [ˌdiːˈseləreɪt] | v. | 降低运行速度 | allow | [əˈlaʊ] | v. | 允许 |

dizziness	['dɪzinəs]	n.	头晕	restricted	[rɪ'strɪktɪd]	adj.	受限制的
electronic	[ɪˌlek'trɒnɪk]	adj.	电子的	Kawasaki	[ˌkawa'saki]	n.	川崎市
awesome	['ɔːsəm]	adj.	令人惊叹的				

C 2 Water dispenser (饮用水)

C: I'm sorry, sir. The tap water cannot be drunk directly.

P: Do you have hot water on the train?

C: Yes, drinking water is available for 24 hours.

P: Would you please tell me where I can get drinking water?

C: There is a water-heater at the end of each carriage offering free boiled water.

P: And do you have cups?

C: There are prepared paper cups beside the water-heater so it doesn't matter if you have cups. I'll show you if you like.

P: All right. I'm afraid I don't know how to use it.

C: Here we are. There are three indicator lights. A red light indicates that the heater is working, and a green light shows that the water has boiled. You can put your cup under the tap and press the big red button to get hot water, but you'd better get a half full avoiding being hurt by hot water especially when the train is moving.

P: Thank you.

Word Tips

tap	[tæp]	n.	水龙头	indicator	['ɪndɪkeɪtə]	n.	指示信号
carriage	['kærɪdʒ]	n.	车厢	press	[pres]	v.	按；压
boil	[bɔɪl]	v.	煮沸	water-heater			热水器

Task 2 Read and role-play the conversations in pairs.

A=Passenger A   **B**=Passenger B   **C**=Train crew member   **P**=Passenger

C 1

C: Good morning, sir. Is this your handbag?

P: Yes, it is. What is the matter?

C: The table is a little bit dirty. I need to clean it up.

P: Ok, thank you.

C: Here is a trash bag. You can put fruit peel, egg shells and sunflower seed shells into it.

P: I see.

C: Excuse me, would you please move your feet aside so I can sweep the floor?

P: Of course.

C: (After 10 seconds) Thank you for your cooperation. Is this your suitcase?

P: Yes. What's wrong with it? Do you want to check it?

C: Not really. I just want to say that it is too big, and may slide down from the rack at any time. Could you please put it under the seat? The top racks are for light luggage. Heavy ones can be stored below the seat or the storage space at both ends of the carriage. Oversize luggage shall always be put in storage space. Please take good care of your valuable and fragile articles.

P: Thank you. You are so considerate.

C: Sure. Let me give you a hand.

P: I can manage it by myself. Thank you all the same.

C: You are welcome.

C 2

P: Excuse me. Where is the toilet?

C: There is a toilet at each end of the car.

P: Is it locked now? It seems that it is occupied for quite a while.

C: I am afraid all the toilets are locked now.

P: Why?

C: According to the regulation, toilets should not be in service when trains stop at a station.

P: Oh, I see. How long will the train stay at the station?

C: Just 5 minutes. The toilet will be available after the train departs.

P: Got it. Thank you.

C 3

A: Excuse me. Where can I find seat 4A?

C: Just go ahead to the eighth row. It's the seat next to the window on your right.

A: But there are a lady and a baby there already.

C: Really? Let's have a look. (to the lady) Excuse me, madam? Is this your seat?

B: Sorry, I have taken the wrong seat. My seat is 4B, the aisle seat. But you see I have a baby with me so it will be very helpful if I can have a seat by the window.

C: (to A)Would you like to change seats with the lady, Sir?

A: That's ok. Lady first.

C: Thank you so much.

C: What is your destination, madam?

B: I am going to Shijiazhuang.

C: The gentleman's destination is Beijing. So you can give the seat back to the gentlemen after the train arrives at Shijiazhuang station.

C 4

A: Excuse me. Do you know how to access internet on the train?

B: I don't know about that.

A: Is there Wi-Fi on the train?

C: There is no wireless network on this train.

A: There is no wireless network on the high-speed trains?

C: Some trains have it, but there is no Wi-Fi service on this train yet.

A: I see. Thank you.

C 5

C: Good afternoon. I'm the conductor of this sleeping car. If you need help, please let me know at any time.

P: All right. Thank you.

C: Can I have a look at your ID card? I'll check the ticket.

P: Ok, here it is. By the way, do we still need to change a ticket voucher on the sleeping car?

C: No. Instead of using ticket voucher to remind your arrival, I will wake you up in time before you arrive at your destination. Here is your ID card.

P: Ok, I see. Thank you. When will the lights be turned off in the evening?

C: At 10: 00 p.m. But there are bedside lamps that you can use.

P: Thank you.

Task 3 Situational practice

Situation 1: Suppose you are a train crew member on the train. You need to make an introduction announcement of the train schedule to passengers according to the following information. What does he/she say?

Train: D253.

Route: From Tianjin to Guangzhou, passing through 16 cities.

Situation 2: Suppose you are a train crew member on the train. Sometimes difficult situations with passengers get out of control. Passengers become aggressive, insulting or drunk and refuse to do what they are asked. What are your procedures for dealing with really disruptive passengers? What can you do in this situation? Make a conversation with your partner and try to practice it.

Task 4 Additional practice: phonetics (Nasals)

1. Pronunciation methods

[m]

发[m]音的常见字母与字母组合有m、mm。

发音方法：双唇鼻辅音。发音时软腭下垂，双唇紧闭，气流从鼻腔送出。

[n]

发[n]音的常见字母与字母组合有n、nn。

发音方法：舌尖齿龈鼻辅音。发音时双唇微微张开，舌尖抵上齿龈，软腭下垂，气流从鼻腔送出。

[ŋ]

发[ŋ]音的常见字母与字母组合有n、ng。

发音方法：舌后软腭鼻辅音。发音时双唇张开，舌尖抵下齿龈，软腭下垂，堵住口腔通道，气流从鼻腔送出，声带振动。

2. Read and practice

[m]	manage	motor	time	mouth	comb	thumb
[n]	attend	name	number	knock	knife	sign
[ŋ]	function	sign	sing	ink	riding	passing

Reading

Train Crew Members Duties and Tasks

The people who works on trains has a variety of jobs. Each member of a train crew has a very specific function. They are responsible for trains to operate as smoothly as possible. They interact with customers in various ways before, during, and after a train ride. What they do aims to attend to passenger needs, questions, and safety. Their professional characteristics include fixed working mode, narrow working environment, irregular diet, working on the train year after year, and going back and forth on the same line, even nights, weekends and holidays. Their core tasks are as follows:

1. Inspect the train for damages before departing, record any interior problems and request repairments if needed.

2. Collect tickets, fares, and sell tickets to passengers in need.

3. Assist passengers with luggage.

4. Answer questions concerning train rules, stations, and timetable information.

5. Assist them with anything (seat location, luggage loading and storage and any special needs they may have while riding the train).

6. Keep the carriage clean.

7. Adjust controls to regulate air-conditioning, heating, and lighting on train for comfort of passengers.

8. Keep the peace by managing disruptive passengers.

9. Dealing with passengers' complaints.

10. Make schedule announcements.

11. Open and close train doors.

12. Get off the train in advance and schedule the exit, assist passengers to board and leave train.

Words and Expressions

variety	[vəˈraɪəti]	n.	不同种类	repairment	[riːˈpeɪmənts]	n.	修理
specific	[spəˈsɪfɪk]	adj.	特有的	fare	[feəz]	n.	车费
responsible	[rɪˈspɒnsəbl]	adj.	有责任的	assist	[əˈsɪst]	v.	帮助
operate	[ˈɒpəreɪt]	v.	运行	concern	[kənˈsɜːn]	v.	涉及
interact	[ˌɪntərˈækt]	v.	交流	load	[ləʊd]	n.	装载量
various	[ˈveəriəs]	adj.	各种不同的	storage	[ˈstɔːrɪdʒ]	n.	存储
ride	[raɪd]	n.	短途旅程	control	[kənˈtrəʊl]	n.	控制装置
attend	[əˈtend]	v.	照顾；接待	regulate	[ˈregjuleɪt]	v.	控制
professional	[prəˈfeʃənl]	adj.	职业的	manage	[ˈmænɪdʒ]	v.	能解决(问题)
characteristic	[ˌkærəktəˈrɪstɪk]	n.	特点	disruptive	[dɪsˈrʌptɪv]	adj.	引起混乱的
fixed	[fɪkst]	adj.	固定的	schedule	[ˈʃedjuːl]	n.	日程安排
irregular	[ɪˈregjələ(r)]	adj.	不规则的	a variety of			各种各样
core	[kɔː(r)]	adj.	最重要的	back and forth			来回
inspect	[ɪnˈspekt]	v.	检查	luggage loading			行李装运
interior	[ɪnˈtɪəriə(r)]	n.	内部	deal with			处理

Task 1 Read the text and decide whether the following statements are **T** (true) or **F** (false).

(　　) 1. Passenger train crew members have a rest at regular time.

(　　) 2. Train crew employees serve the passengers throughout the train journey.

(　　) 3. Passengers' luggage can be placed on racks of the train with the help of the crewmen.

(　　) 4. The crewmen have no right to sell tickets to passengers.

(　　) 5. Train crew should assist passengers with their needs.

Task 2 Translate the following sentences into Chinese.

1. Each member of a train crew has a very specific function.

_____

2. Assist passengers with luggage.

_____

3. Keep the peace by managing disruptive passengers.
_____

4. Dealing with passengers' complaints.
_____

5. Get off the train in advance and schedule the exit, assist passengers to board and leave train.
_____

Task 3 Fill in the blanks according to the Chinese meanings.

Luggage Missing Service

The places where goods are most likely to be lost on high-speed trains are the entrance, _____ (行李架), seats, washrooms and dining car. Once you find that you have lost something on the train, you can _____(仔细搜索) these places. You can also _____ (向服务员寻求帮助). If you find that you have lost something after disembarking from the train, you can _____(填写丢失行李表格) on the official ticket website 12306.cn and _____(等待回复). Usually, you can get the answer within 6 hours.

Task 1 Collect information about warm service on high-speed trains, then discuss in groups the details about service on high-speed trains and have better preparation about the train trip. Make a report about the services in English within each group. You can refer to the Task 2.

Table of contents
1. Board and disembark guidance
2. Broadcast service
3. Language service
4. Food & drink service
5. Free service for business class seat
6. Service for special passengers
7. Cleaning service
8. Luggage missing service
9. Emergency service

Task 2 Match the English in column A with their corresponding Chinese in column B.

A	B
The express train will run from Tianjin to Beijing without any stops in between.	无论您何时需要帮助，请告诉我。
The toilet is occupied. Please wait for a moment.	这趟特快列车将从天津直达北京，中途不停靠。

A	B
Please keep quiet on the train.	卫生间现在有人，请稍等。
The train will arrive at Tianjin at fifteen past nine.	列车将在九点一刻到达天津。
Whenever you need help, please let me know.	在列车上请保持安静。

Knowledge Stock

1. Common facilities on the high-speed train

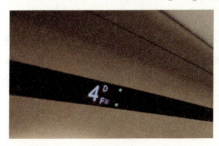

Seat screen

Luggage closets

Power socket

Water dispenser

Dustbins

Disposal bag

Dining car

LCD TV sets

Western-style toilets

2. Toilet sign on Chinese High-speed Railway

(1) "Green" or "Red" light

You can check the LED sign above the door for the availability of the washroom in your carriage. If it is a "green" light, it means there is nobody (无人) in the washroom; and if it is "red" or "yellow" light, it means the washroom is occupied (有人). Not all the signs use the "green" or "red" light, some trains use Chinese words "有人" or "无人" to describe the availability.

(2) Male or female

On the door of the washroom, it has the sign for male (男) or female (女). Usually, the washroom on the train are for use by both female and male, and no special distinction.

(3) Squat toilet or western style toilet

Some trains offer both squat toilets (蹲厕) and western style toilets (马桶). You can tell by the sign on the door of the washroom and choose the one you are used to.

(4) Unlock or lock

"开" means "unlock" and "关" means "lock". Toggle button is available on the door. When you get into the washroom, rotate the button from "unlock" to "lock". Then, the door will be locked which means someone else could not enter. When you finished using the toilet, rotate the button from "lock" to "unlock".

Unit 11 Dining Service

Goals

Be familiar with the useful expressions about serving food;
Know how to recommend specialties and take orders;
Know how to serve in the dining car;
Grasp the English names of dishes.

Warming-up

Try to think

Task 1 Match the words and expressions with the pictures.

Fruits in seasons	Regional food	Leisure food
Dessert	Boxed meals	Soft drinks
Local beers	Local specialties	Western meals

1._____

2._____

3._____

4._____

5._____

6._____

7._____ 8._____ 9._____

Task 2 Classify the food above on the basis of a temperature-controlled supply chain.

1. Cold-chain food _____
2. Hot food _____
3. Food at room temperature _____
4. Frozen food _____

Try to listen

The High-speed Railway broadcasting

Task 1 Listen carefully and fill in the blanks with what you hear.

Ladies and gentlemen, welcome aboard the CRH train. _____ facilities are available for you to board the train. The _____ car is in the middle of the train and will offer a variety of foods and _____ meals. Passengers are welcome to visit. Electric water dispensers and _____ rooms are provided in each coach. Please be cautious when using water dispensers and do not throw any _____ into the toilets.

Task 2 Read the paragraph in Task 1 loudly and try to recite it.

Task 1 Retell the conversations below and imitate the pronunciation and intonation after listening to the recording.

C 1　The location of dining car (指引餐车位置)

C=Train crew member　　P=Passenger

P: Excuse me, is there a dining car on this train?
C: Yes, it is carriage 5.
P: Great. How can I get there?
C: Take this way, it is 2 cars away.
P: I want to get some night snack. Is it still available at this time?
C: Yes. Food is served all day 24 hours.
P: Do I have to make a reservation?

C: No. You don't have to. It almost always has tables available. You can walk in anytime.

P: Ok. Thank you very much.

C: You're welcome.

C 2　How to get takeout (如何取外卖)

A=Train attendant　P=Passenger

P: Hello, I've ordered takeout. But I didn't get it at the Nanchang stop. Do you know how I can get it?

A: I can get your takeout in the dining car.

P: Ok, thanks.

A: (in the dining car) Sir, how can I help you?

P: I would like to get my takeout.

A: Did you order it online?

P: Yes.

A: Ok. May I have the last 4 digits of your phone number? I need it to look for the order.

P: Sure. It is 1346.

A: Ok. I think I find it.

P: Good!

A: Sir, your food is here already. We will bring it to your seat shortly.

P: Great. Thank you.

Task 2　Read and role-play the conversations in pairs.

C 1

A: Good morning, madam. How can I help you?

P: Are these cookies free?

A: No, they are not. Is there anything you would like to have?

P: Let me think... Do you serve drinks?

A: Yes. We have mineral water, orange juice, red tea and coffee. Which one do you like?

P: A bottle of orange juice, please.

A: Here you are.

P: May I have a straw?

A: Sorry, we don't have straws.

105

C 2

P: Excuse me, do you offer meals on the train?

A: I'm sorry. We don't serve meals because this is a short-distance train. However, you can get some snacks and drinks in the dining bar anytime.

P: Do you know what snacks and drinks are available?

A: There is a good selections in the dining bar such as black tea, milk tea, green tea, coffee, coca cola, sprite, beer, red bull, Wong Lo Kat, soybean milk, soda water, mineral water, ice cream, potato chips, biscuits, cake, peanut, grape, pears, oranges, apples, cherry tomato, and so on.

P: Sounds good. I'll go to the dinning bar and grab something.

A: Enjoy!

C 3

A: Can I take your order now, madam?

P: Yes. Any recommendation?

A: Beef curry is great. The two side dishes are tasty as well. It also comes with soup of the day.

P: It sounds good. I'll try it.

A: Anything else?

P: Is there any good local dishes?

A: Would you like to try Xi'an typical snack foods? They are good.

P: Hmm... (on a second though) I think I will have one Chinese hamburger, and one crude pancake in mutton soup instead.

A: Sure. Anything else?

P: No. That's all.

A: Any drinks?

P: Just a bottle of water. Thanks.

Word Tips

curry	['kʌri]	n.	咖喱菜	crude	[kru:d]	n.	未经加工的
pancake	['pænkeɪk]	n.	烙饼	mutton	['mʌtn]	n.	羊肉

Task 3 Situational practice

Situation 1: Suppose you are a train attendant. A foreigner wants to order supper and a cup of coffee in the dining car. You offer help to her/him. Make a conversation with your partner and practice it. The following is for your reference.

Price:

Instant coffee: ¥10/cup, ¥15/bottle, ¥10/tin.

Situation 2: Suppose you are selling food on the train. A foreigner wants to have some specialties for lunch. Briefly introduce the dishes on the menu and recommend the specialties to him/her. Make a conversation with your partner and practice it.

Task 4　Additional practice: phonetics (Laterals & semivowels)

1. Pronunciation methods

[l]

发[l]音的常见字母与字母组合有l、ll。

发音方法：舌端齿龈边辅音。发音时舌尖及舌端紧贴上齿龈，舌前向硬腭抬起，气流从舌的旁边送出。当此音为尾音时，将舌端抵住上齿龈，舌前下陷，舌后上抬，舌面形成凹形。[l]为浊辅音，声带振动。

[w]

发[w]音的常见字母与字母组合有w、wh、u、o。

发音方法：舌后软腭半元音。发音时舌后部向软腭抬起，舌位高。双唇收小并向前突出，声带振动。发音短促，立刻滑向其后的元音。

[j]

发[j]音的常见字母有y、u、i。

发音方法：舌前硬腭半元音。发音时舌前部向硬腭尽量抬起，舌位较高，双唇伸展成扁平状。[j]为浊辅音，声带振动。

2. Read and practice

[l]	lunch	online	locker	luggage	outlet	wallet
	mineral	rail	local	mobile	hall	specialty
[w]	what	wallet	quality	quite	one	once
[j]	yellow	your	yes	cue	use	view

A Bite of High-speed Railway Journey

Starting from July 17, 2017, high-speed trains can offer on-demand food delivery service through website 12306.cn and its App two hours before the train arrives at the station.

Since January 18, 2018, China Rail has minimized the food servicing time between the source of the food's production and the passengers' door from 2 hours to 1 hour and launched the local specialties online pre-ordering service.

You can not only order food provided by the trains but also by other restaurants near the railway stations, such as fast food chains including KFC, McDonald's, Burger King, Dicos, or local specialties and halal food available for set menus, depending on the train routes. The train attendants will pick up the meal and deliver it to your seat. So far, the orders can be made one hours prior to departure via WeChat except China Rail's official website or its App.

Since January 21, 2019, some high-speed trains started using online ordering service that make the food ordering process even easier. Passengers just need to

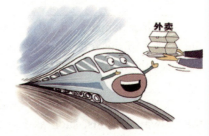

scan the QR code on the seat and place an order, the attendants will deliver the food to your seat. You can choose onboard options either online or through the official railway App for a meal order now. It greatly improved customers experience. Passengers don't need to walk through carriages to find the dining car and check what meals are served.

Passengers now have more food and beverage options to fit their various needs. Meal selections and service in the high-speed train continue to improve for better customer experience.

Words and Expressions

bite	[baɪt]	n.	咬；一口	scan	[skæn]	v.	扫描
delivery	[dɪˈlɪvəri]	n.	递送	option	[ˈɒpʃn]	n.	选择
minimize	[ˈmɪnɪmaɪz]	v.	减少到最低程度	set menu			套餐
launch	[lɔːntʃ]	v.	推出	pick up			领取
specialty	[ˈspeʃəlti]	n.	特色食品	prior to			在……之前
halal	[həˈlæl]	adj.	清真的	on-demand			按需
attendant	[əˈtendənt]	n.	服务员	scan the QR code			扫QR码
prior	[ˈpraɪə(r)]	adj.	在前面的	onboard options			列车自营餐品

Task 1 Choose the best answer.

1. On a High-speed Railway journey, you can pre-order food _____.
   A. at dining car　　　　B. online　　　　C. both of them
2. Halal food is provided depending on _____.
   A. the train types　　　B. the train routes　　C. the train service
3. You must place the order and pay at least _____ hours before the train leaves.
   A. 1　　　　　　　　B. 2　　　　　　　C. 3
4. Takeout is delivered to the passengers by _____.
   A. a food deliver guy　　B. a train attendant　　C. themselves
5. Passengers can pre-order their onboard meals without going to dining car since _____.
   A. 2018　　　　　　　B. 2019　　　　　　C. 2017

Task 2 Translate the following sentences into Chinese.

1. Starting from July 17, 2017, high-speed trains can offer on-demand food delivery service through website 12306.cn and its App two hours before the train arrives at the station.

_____

2. Since January 18, 2018, China Rail has minimized the food servicing time between the source of the food's production and the passengers' door from 2 hours to 1 hour and launched the local specialties online pre-ordering service.

_____

3. You can not only order food provided by the trains but also by other restaurants near the railway stations, such as fast food chain including KFC, McDonald's, Burger King,

Dicos, or local specialties and halal food available for set menus, depending on the train routes.

_____

4. Passengers don't need to walk through carriages to find the dining car and check what meals are served.

_____

5. Meal selections and service in the high-speed train continue to improve for better customer experience.

_____

Task 3 The following is the process of ordering takeout through 12306 mobile App. Put the following steps in the correct order.

A. Enter your train number to confirm participating stations on your route and stores that can provide food service, sorted by station.
B. Click the store to see food options available, make your selections and click "提交订单".
C. Choose the means of payment and submit the payment to complete your order.
D. Opt for the time and the passing station.
E. After entering the main screen, click "catering specialty" in the menu bar below.
F. Enter your seat number and click "立即支付" for next step.
G. Open 12306 mobile App and create or login your account.
Correct order: _____

Task 1 The picture on the right is high-speed train trips from Beijing to Xi'an and from Xi'an to Shanghai. Choose one of the passing stations along the route to take a simulated ordering online via 12306.cn or its App. Work in groups.

Task 2 Chose one of restaurants and make a good Chinese and English bilingual menu.

1. The process of how the takeout is delivered to you

(1) Use your phone to order takeout via 12306 mobile App.

(2) The delivery men pick up orders at restaurants near the stations, then take them to the platforms and give them to the train attendants.

(3) The train attendants take the order from the delivery men, and complete the delivery by taking the meal to the passenger's seat.

2. Common food on high-speed trains

When traveling on a Chinese train, the food can be bought from the dining car, the food trolleys, and the platform vendors. The fare of the food is not included in the train ticket and only Chinese Yuan, WeChat Pay and Alipay are accepted for payment. Generally, the food price is higher than that of the outside restaurants or stores. If possible, you can bring some on your own, like hamburger, bread, fruit, or the most popular instant noodles among Chinese passengers. Food delivery service is available on some high-speed trains, but one needs to read Chinese to use it.

Drinks

milk tea 奶茶	mineral water 矿泉水
red bull 红牛	black tea 红茶
Wong Lo Kat 王老吉	green tea 绿茶
soybean milk 豆浆	orange juice 鲜橙多
soda water 苏打水	instant coffee 速溶咖啡
milk 牛奶	coca cola 可乐
sprite 雪碧	beer 啤酒

Snacks

peanuts 花生	pistachio 开心果
crackers 薄脆饼干	potato chips 炸马铃薯片
cake 蛋糕	raisins 葡萄干
biscuits 饼干	beef jerky 牛肉干
fruits 水果	sunflower seeds 瓜子
ice cream 冰激凌	fish jerky 鱼片
cherry tomato 圣女果	haw slices 山楂片
vacuum packed braised food 真空包装的红烧食品	18th Street Fried Dough Twists 18街麻花

Main Dishes

beef brisket 牛腩饭	hot dry noodles 热干面
pork chop 猪排饭	porridge 粥
spicy diced chicken 辣子鸡丁	pickles 咸菜
vegetables 蔬菜	boiled eggs 水煮鸡蛋
steak with pepper sauce 黑胡椒牛排	Chinese breads 中式包点
steamed pork with preserved vegetable 青菜蒸肉饭	steamed stuff buns with pork fillings 猪肉馅包子
steamed pork with brown sauce 红烧蒸肉	spicy diced chicken with peanuts 宫保鸡丁
beef curry 咖喱牛肉饭	tomato and egg soup 西红柿鸡蛋汤

3. Particular items available at specific stations

Lanzhou	hand-pulled noodles with beef	Xi'an	marinated meat in baked bun (Roujiamo)
Tangshan	fried chestnuts	Tianjin	Goubuli steamed stuffed buns
Fuzhou	steamed dumpling	Guilin	rice noodles
Xiangyang	roast fish	Shangrao	braised chicken leg
Dezhou	braised chicken	Kumul	Hami melon
Wuxi	fried spare ribs	Litang	lotus roots soup
Zaozhuang	vegetable with pancake	Yongzhou	stewed ribs with seaweeds
Jiaxing	Zongzi (pyramid-shaped dumplings made of glutinous rice and wrapped in bamboo or reed leaves)	Wuhan/Wuchang	braised duck neck, hot noodles with sesame paste, roast chicken, fried Wuchang fish

Section IV
Special and Emergency Service

Unit 12 Special and Emergency Service

Goals

Be familiar with the English expressions of diseases and facilities;
Grasp the useful expressions of special and emergency services;
Learn to deal with different emergencies;
Learn about the First Aid basics.

Warming-up

Try to think

Task 1 Match the words and expressions with the pictures.

SOS button	Emergency hammer	Emergency braking
Emergency exit	Emergency unlock button	Fire extinguisher
Inner end door	A platform compensator	Emergency alarm & fire alarm

1._____

2._____

3._____

4._____

5._____

6._____

7._____ 8._____ 9._____

Task 2　Fill in the blanks with proper words and expressions.

Try to listen

The High-speed Railway broadcasting

Task 1　Listen carefully and fill in the blanks with what you hear.

　　Dear passengers, due to some mechanical _____ of the central _____ system, the train doors will be _____ manually. Please do not block the _____ or gather at the _____. The train attendants will open the door for you. We ask for your cooperation and understanding.

Task 2　Read the paragraph in Task 1 loudly and recite it.

Task 1　Retell the conversations below and imitate the pronunciation and intonation after listening to the recordings.

C 1　**The disabled on board** (残障旅客乘车)

C=Train crew member　P=Passenger

P: Excuse me, are there access and seats designated for passengers with wheelchairs?
C: Yes. There is a wheelchair access in carriage 5.

P: Thanks. Where can I store the wheelchair once boarded?
C: You can leave it at the left luggage space next to entrance and make sure it won't move away. I will affix it shortly.
P: Sure. Thanks!

Word Tips

wheelchair	['wi:ltʃeə(r)]	n.	轮椅	affix	[ə'fɪks]	v.	(使)固定

C 2 Baby care washroom (母婴室)

C: May I help you, madam?
P: Is there a baby care room?
C: No, there is no baby care room on high-speed trains. There is however a foldable table for diaper changing or baby nursing in barrier-free washroom.
P: Where is it?
C: It is at the end of carriage 5. I'll show you the way.
P: Ok. Thank you.
C: It seems that the room is occupied.
C: Hello, anybody inside? I think there is nobody inside. You can use it.
P: But I can't open the door?
C: Ok. Please press the round green button, and the door will open automatically. When you get into the washroom, rotate the button from "unlock" to "lock".
P: Oh, thank you!

Word Tips

diaper	['daɪpə(r)]	n.	尿布	occupied	['ɒkjupaɪd]	adj.	使用中的
barrier	['bæriə(r)]	n.	障碍	rotate	[rəʊ'teɪt]	v.	(使)旋转

Task 2　Read and role-play the conversations in pairs.

C 1

C: May I help you, Madam?

P: I just put a cup of hot water on the tray table. My daughter accidentally spilled the water and got burned on her hand.

C: Oh, no. Let me have a look. Does it hurt a lot?

P: I have cooled the burns under running cool water to reduce her pain, but she still feels a lot pain. Is there an ice pack?

C: Ice is a no-no. It makes you feel better temporarily, but could deepen the burn. The skin turns red. It must be painful. Don't worry. It's a minor injury. I will get the First Aid Kit for you.

P: Thank you very much!

C: Sure. I will be right back.

C 2

P: Excuse me, what is the matter? Why did the train slow down?

C: Don't worry. The heavy snow covered the High-speed Railway routes, so the train is running in a limited speed.

P: I see. Can we still arrive in Shenyangbei on time?

C: The train will be delayed for some time. Sorry about the delay and inconvenience.

P: That is all right. Do you know what time we can arrive at the Shenyangbei Station?

C: It is very hard to tell now, and I will let you know once we have the timetable.

C 3

C: Whose kid is running on the corridor?

P: Oh, she's my daughter. She's excited. This is her first time to be on a train.

C: Of course, it is going to be a fun trip for her. The train is going to stop. Please have her sit down so that she won't fall accidentally.

P: Sure, I will.

C: Why is your son crying? Is there anything I can help?

P: Oh... He is just bored.

C: You may want to have some toys and snacks next time for them. It is a long trip for kids.

P: I did prepare some snacks and toys for them but I forgot them in the car.

C: It happens all the time. Let me know if you need any help.

P: Okay, thank you.

C 4

C: Dear passengers, attention please. Due to the system fault, the train cannot run normally. The rescue train will arrive at 10:20, please wait patiently. You can transfer onto the rescue train on the opposite side of the same platform. Please follow our crew members taking your belongings with you and take your seats with the same numbers when you get on the train. We appreciate your patience and understanding on this matter.

P: Excuse me, my ticket is business class seat.

C: Due to different train models, you may not be able to take a business seat on the new train. If you need to refund the price difference, please contact the train crew for the passenger record. You can get a refund at station after leaving the train.

P: Will the train stop at Hangzhouxi?

C: Don't worry. The speed, route and stops of that train are the same with this one.

P: You can report the information of transfer, so we can timely connect with the station and deal with the handover procedures. We also supply 600 emergency meals to meet the dietary needs of passengers.

C: I see. Thank you.

P: You are welcome.

Task 3 Situational practice

Situation 1: Suppose you are a train crew member. A passenger's leg is broken. He/she requests wheelchair service. You offer help to him/her. Where is the wheelchair? How does he/she get the wheelchair? Make a conversation with your partner and try to practice it.

Situation 2: Suppose you are a train crew member. A passenger complained the air conditioner doesn't work. You offer help to him/her. Why doesn't the air conditioner work and when it will work? Make a conversation with your partner and try to practice it.

Task 4 Additional practice: phonetics (Incomplete plosion)

1. Pronunciation methods

失去爆破：当一个爆破音后面紧跟着另一个爆破音时，前面的爆破音不发生爆破。

发音方法：对于前一个爆破音，只做发音的姿势，刚要发出时，立即发出第二个爆破音。这种现象叫作失去爆破。

不完全爆破：当一个爆破音后面紧跟着一个摩擦音、破擦音、鼻辅音或舌边音时，前面的爆破音只作部分爆破。

发音方法：对于前一个爆破音，做好发音的姿势，刚发出时，立即过渡到第二个摩擦音或破擦音上去。第一个爆破音发出的声音是非常轻微的，有时甚至听不出来。这种现象叫作不完全爆破。

2. Read and practice

爆破音+爆破音	kept	next door	sharp pencil	big kite
爆破音+摩擦音	success	old friends	just then	folk songs
爆破音+破擦音	object	a fast train	great changes	that joke
爆破音+舌边音	badly	I'd like to	straight line	at last
爆破音+鼻辅音	midnight	help me	not now	a different meaning

First Aid Basics—ABCs

A well-prepared First Aid Kit is an important tool in treating minor injuries that commonly occur daily. A well-prepared First Aid Kit can help to reduce the severity of the injury, prevent infection and even deal with emergencies. First Aid is as easy as ABC-airway, breathing and CPR (Cardiopulmonary Resuscitation). In emergency situations, there are three basic C's rules, including checking the danger scene, calling for professional help and caring for the victims.

In case a person is unconscious and not breathing, CPR should be started quickly. The following is CPR steps:

1. Tap or shake the person on the shoulder and shout to him or her "Are you ok?"
2. Call for professional assistance.
3. Ensure the person to lie on his or her back and kneel beside him or her.
4. Open the airway. Tilt the head back slightly to lift the chin.
5. Check for breathing. Listen carefully for sounds of breathing.
6. Compress chest 30 times.
7. Give two rescue breaths.
8. Repeat the cycle of 30 chest compressions and two rescue breaths.

Words and Expressions

aid	[eɪd]	n.	援助；帮助
kit	[kɪt]	v.	成套工具
treat	[tri:t]	v.	治疗
minor	['maɪnə(r)]	adj.	较小的
injury	['ɪndʒəri]	n.	(对躯体的)伤害；损伤
occur	[ə'kɜ:(r)]	v.	发生
reduce	[rɪ'dju:s]	v.	减少
severity	[sɪ'verəti]	n.	严重
infection	[ɪn'fekʃn]	n.	传染
cardiopulmonary	[ˌkɑrdioʊ'pʊlməˌnɛri]	adj	心肺的
resuscitation	[rɪˌsʌsɪ'teɪʃn]	n.	复活
scene	[si:n]	n	(尤指不愉快事件发生的)地点
victim	['vɪktɪm]	n.	受害者
unconscious	[ʌn'kɒnʃəs]	adj.	无知觉的；昏迷的
tap	[tæp]	n.	轻拍；轻敲

assistance	[əˈsɪstəns]	n.	帮助
airway	[ˈeəweɪ]	n.	气道
slightly	[ˈslaɪtli]	adv.	略微
lift	[lɪft]	v.	(被)提起，举起
chin	[tʃɪn]	n.	颏；下巴
compress	[kəmˈpres]	v.	压紧；压缩
rescue	[ˈreskju:]	v.	抢救
care for			照顾

Task 1 Read the text and decide whether the following statements are **T** (true) or **F** (false).

(　　) 1. Basic First Aid can help to deal with emergence.
(　　) 2. If a person is not responding to you, but still breathing, begin CPR.
(　　) 3. The ABCs of CPR are airway, breathing and compressing.
(　　) 4. Tilt the head back slightly to lift the chin, aiming to open the airway.
(　　) 5. Perform 30 chest compressions, followed by two breaths.

Task 2 Translate the following sentences into Chinese.

1. A well-prepared First Aid Kit can help to reduce the severity of the injury, prevent infection and even deal with emergencies.
_____

2. First Aid is as easy as ABC-airway, breathing and CPR (Cardiopulmonary Resuscitation).
_____

3. In emergency situations, there are three basic C's rules, including checking the danger scene, calling for professional help and caring for the victims.
_____

4. Open the airway. Tilt the head back slightly to lift the chin.
_____

5. Repeat the cycle of 30 chest compressions and two rescue breaths.
_____

Task 3 Fill in the blanks according to the Chinese meanings.

Train Travel Tips During the Coronavirus Outbreak Period

If you are already in China and need to take a train, precautions need to be taken to _____(保护) yourself.

1. Wear a _____ (口罩).
2. Wash your hands frequently with _____ (肥皂) or hand sanitizer and water for at least 20 seconds.
3. Avoid touching your eyes, _____(鼻子), and mouth before washing your hands.
4. Take your own hand sanitizer and disposable _____(湿巾) with you.

Group Work

Task 1 What if a fire occurs in a high-speed train? Discuss how to deal with the fire. Put the following steps of operating portable fire extinguisher in the correct order. Then choose one of the emergency situations in Task 2 and make a performance in English according to its procedures within each group.

A. If fire is not readily controllable, evacuate car immediately.

B. Approach fire at a close, but safe distance, ensure you have an escape route behind you, remove safety pin and test extinguisher.

C. Spray in side to side motion until fire is extinguished (average discharge time is 8 seconds).

D. Report discharge of extinguisher on defect form.

E. Locate and remove fire extinguisher from its housing.

F. Crouch down to better see the flames and to avoid smoke inhalation.

G. Aim nozzle at base of fire and activate the extinguisher.

H. Verify by gauge that it is charged.

Correct order：_____

Task 2 Match the English in column A with their corresponding Chinese in column B.

A	B
Fire or smoke in a train way, station, or vehicle	列车疏散
Passenger collapse or falls on a vehicle or in a station	列车突然停车
Sudden stop by vehicle	列车、车站或车辆内的火灾或烟雾
Train derailment/collision	生病、受伤或死亡
Total power failure	断电
Train evacuation	自然灾害（大风、洪水、地震等）
Sickness, injuries or fatalities	旅客在车上或车站内摔倒、坠落
Natural disasters (high winds, flood, earthquake, etc.)	列车脱轨/碰撞

1. **In China, the following passengers are considered special care travelers:**
- The elderly—age limit: 70 and above;
- The very young—for kids traveling for free with their parents;
- The ill;

- The injured;
- The pregnant;
- The deaf and dumb;
- People using a wheelchair;
- People with disabilities;
- The blind.

2. Common medical vocabulary—some symptoms and possible problems

toothache	牙疼	headache	头疼
nauseous	恶心	stomachache	胃痛
bleed	流血	loose bowels	拉肚子
broken bones	骨折	vomit	呕吐
scald	烫伤	dizzy	头晕
diarrhea	腹泻	car sickness	晕车
have a cold/fever	发烧	high blood pressure	高血压
asthma	哮喘	heart attack	心脏病发作

- Her head hurts!
- His ears are sore!
- I have a toothache!
- My arm is sore!
- I cut my finger!
- My nose is runny!
- My chest feels tight!
- My stomach hurts!
- My legs feel weak!
- I twisted my ankle!
- This passenger suffered broken bones and his leg is bleeding.
- His nose is constantly running. He had a fever and got a headache.
- Tom caught a cold. He vomited a few times. He got a stomachache and had loose bowels.
- My uncle died of high blood pressure.
- A passenger scalded her hand with boiling water.
- She felt dizzy and nauseous.
- We have some medicine for car sickness, colds and diarrhea.

- Her daughter suffered a serious heart attack.

3. When riding on/off an escalator or moving walkway:

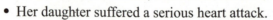

- Always hold the handrail;
- Always face forwards;
- Stand firm and don't walk;
- Stand clear of the edges of steps;
- Always watch your steps if wearing sandals or slippers;
- Do not lean against the sides or rest on the handrail;
- Do not sit on the escalator steps;

- Do not run, play or jump;
- Take extra care when stepping off.

4. When stepping off an escalator or moving walkway:

- Step off promptly;
- Move away from the landing area immediately.

5. General safety guidelines:

- Look after children and offer assistance to the elderly;
- Always use the lift if carrying bulky baggage, using a baby pushchair, or a wheelchair;
- Do not carry any excessively long object;
- Keep your feet clear of the side edges;
- Take extra care when an escalator is stopped and used as a fixed staircase as the height of steps will vary;
- In the event of an accident immediately press the Emergency Stop button.

6. Use the lift if you:

- Are elderly or with children;
- Are mobility impaired or wheelchair users;
- Are traveling with trolleys, baggage, bulky items or have a baby in a baby pram.

7. When using the lift:

- Always give priority to passengers in need;
- Allow passengers to exit before entering;
- Do not overload the lift;
- Stand back and keep your body away from the doors;
- Keep belongings clear of the doors;
- Do not force the lift doors open;
- If the lift stops between floors or the doors fail to open, press the Emergency Alarm button, remain calm and wait for assistance.

Appendix

Appendix 1 High-speed Railway Broadcast

When a high-speed train is going to stop, there will be broadcast announcement that tells the passengers where they are going to arrive. Both Chinese and English are available, making you worry free about missing your arrival station. During the other time of the whole trip, quiet and gentle music will accompany with you.

1. 车站广播

• 请注意！我们正在进行体温测定和公共卫生检查，感谢您的配合。稍后您可以进入候车室休息，我们的车站设有网吧和阅览室，您可以阅览中英文书籍和杂志。

Attention please! We are doing thermal scan to each passenger for the interest of public health. Thank you for your cooperation! Once it is done, you can enter the waiting room. There is an internet bar and a reading room inside, where you can surf the internet, and find some Chinese and English books and magazines.

• 请携带有效旅行证件并确认签注有效。如无法完成内地出境或香港入境手续，可由车站工作人员协助您乘坐就近列车返回内地车站，并办理补票手续，核收手续费。

For a smooth trip, please carry valid travel document with validated endorsement. Passengers failing to go through the mainland exit or Hong Kong entry procedures should take the next train back to the mainland with the assistance of station staff and pay ticket fee and service charge for the trip.

• 各位旅客：由于不利的天气原因，今天部分列车晚点，请关注车站显示屏或公告，或咨询工作人员。因列车晚点给您带来不便，特此向您致歉。

Ladies and gentlemen, some trains will be delayed due to poor weather condition. Please check the information board or ask station staff for updated train schedules. We apologize for the inconvenience.

• 亲爱的旅客：由于车站客流巨大，候车时请不要在椅子上或地上躺卧。为了其他旅客的方便，请您把座位上的行李拿下来。谢谢您的合作，祝您旅途愉快！

Dear passengers, please do not lie on the chairs or floor while waiting for the train because of the huge passenger flow at the station. For other passengers' convenience, please take your luggage down from the seats and leave it on the floor. Thank you for your cooperation. Have a nice trip!

• 各位旅客：为营造诚实守信、文明乘车的良好氛围，请广大旅客自觉买票乘车。对恶意逃票的行为，铁路部门将依法依规予以处理，并根据《征信业管理条例》上报地方征信部门，记入个人信用信息系统。为避免对个人信用造成影响，请需要的旅客及时办理补票手续。

Ladies and gentlemen, please take trains with valid tickets. Passengers with fare evasion will be punished and reported to the credit bureau according to the regulations on the *Administration of the Credit Investigation Industry*. To avoid negative impacts to your personal credit, please buy your ticket as soon as possible if you failed to get one in advance.

2. 关门前提示

• 车门即将关闭，请注意安全。

Attention please, the door is closing.

3. 欢迎词

• 女士们、先生们：欢迎您乘坐高铁动车组列车，我代表动车组全体乘务人员向您问好，祝您旅行愉快。列车运行前方到站是：济南西站。

Ladies and gentlemen, welcome to the High-speed EMU Train. It's my pleasure to extend our best regards to you on behalf of all the crew members. Wish you a pleasant journey. The next stop is Jinanxi Railway Station.

• 亲爱的旅客：欢迎乘坐本次列车，我们全体乘务人员向您问好。请爱护车内设施。如需帮助，可查阅服务指南或咨询乘务人员。

Dear passengers, welcome aboard the train. It's my pleasure to extend our best regards to you on behalf of the crew members. Please take good care of the facilities in the train and refer to the train service guide or consult the crew members for more information.

4. 开车前广播

• 亲爱的旅客：欢迎您乘坐本次列车。请核对车次，并对号入座。随身携带的物品请妥善放置在行李架上或大件行李处，以免掉下砸伤旅客。列车马上就要开车了，非本次列车的旅客请及时下车。

Dear passengers, welcome aboard the train. Please be seated in the assigned seat according to the seat number on your ticket and put your luggage safely on the luggage rack or the designated place at the end of the coach for oversized luggage. The train is leaving. If you boarded the wrong train, please get off as soon as possible. Thanks.

5. 车厢服务

• 女士们、先生们，欢迎您乘坐"复兴号"动车组。担任本次列车服务工作的是中国铁路广州局集团有限公司的乘务组，我代表列车全体工作人员衷心祝福您旅行愉快、一路平安。本次列车由16节车厢组成，2号、15号、16号车厢为一等座车；1号、6号车厢设商务座坐席；餐车设在9号车厢； 8号车厢设有残疾人卫生间及婴儿护理桌。您上车后，请按照车票上的座位号对号入座，随身物品请放在行李架上，较大物品请您放在车厢一端大件行李处，并妥善保管。车厢设有电茶炉，接开水时注意防止烫伤。每节车厢都设有洗手间，您在使用时请勿将杂物丢进便池内。车上电源插座仅限于笔记本电脑、手机、平板电脑、电动剃须刀、移动充电器的充电，请您在充电时注意用电安全。带小孩的旅客请看护好小孩，勿让小孩触碰插座，以免造成意外。本次列车全程禁止吸烟，请不要携带易燃、易爆危险物品上车，如果您携带了易燃、易爆等危险物品上车，请交给列车工作人员妥善保管。在列车正常运行中，请勿碰触车厢内乘客紧急制动手柄等安全设施，不要倚靠在车门上，以免发生意外。列车运行中，请带小孩的旅客看护好小朋友，上下车时请注意列车与站台之间的缝隙。了解更多铁路出行资讯，请关注广州铁路官方微信和官方微博。感谢您乘坐本次列车，祝您旅途愉快。

Ladies and gentlemen, welcome aboard the Fuxing Train. The crew of this trip is from the China Railway Guangzhou Bureau Group Cooperation Limited. It is our pleasure to have you on board. The train consists of 16 coaches. Coach 2, Coach 15 and Coach 16 are the first-class coaches. Coach 1 and Coach 6 are the business class coaches and Coach 9 is the buffet coach. The handicap restroom and infant changing station are in Coach 8. Please be seated according to the seat number on your ticket and put your belongings on the rack above the seats. Please leave bulky or oversized luggage at the designated luggage place at the end of each coach. Electric water dispensers and washing rooms are available in each coach. Be cautious when using the electric water dispensers or taking hot water. Please do not drop any waste into the toilets. The power sockets in the coach are only for charging laptop, mobile phone, tablet PC, electric shaver and portable charger. For passengers traveling with kids, please keep your kids away from the power sockets. Smoking is strictly prohibited during the whole trip. Flammable or explosive articles are not allowed in the train. If you have any of such items, please give them to the train staff for safety concern. We will keep them for you during the trip. Please do not touch any safety devices in the coach or lean on the doors to avoid accidents. Take good care of your children and mind the gap between the train and the platform when getting off. Please pay attention to Guangzhou Railway official Weibo and WeChat for more information. Thank you for taking our train. We wish you a pleasant journey.

• 各位旅客：请注意，列车即将进入高原地区，有些旅客可能会感到轻度不适，比如头痛、胸闷、气短、晕眩和耳鸣，请您不要紧张，放松心情。尽量在座位上不要走动，如需要走动，请慢行。不要吸烟、饮酒和过度饮食，相信您很快就会适应海拔的变化。谢谢！

Ladies and gentlemen, attention please. Our train is entering high altitude areas. Some passengers might experience some uncomfortableness such as headaches, chest tightness, breathing difficulty, dizziness and ear ringing. In this case, please don't be nervous and stay relaxed. Try to remain in your seat or walk slowly if have to. Do not smoke, drink, or overly eat. You would get used to the high altitudes soon. Thank you!

• 餐车位于列车中部。我们为您准备了种类丰富的餐点，需要的旅客可以前去选购。

The dining car is in the middle of the train. We offer a variety of foods and set meals.

• 旅客们：本次列车包卧仍有部分空余铺位。有需要的旅客，可以联系列车工作人员办理。

Dear passengers, there are still some soft sleepers available. Passengers who would like to upgrade their classes, please contact the attendants.

• 旅客们：本次列车普卧仍有部分空余铺位。有需要的旅客，可以联系列车工作人员办理。

Dear passengers, there are still some hard sleepers available. Passengers who would like to upgrade their classes, please contact the attendants.

• 女士们、先生们，目前列车仍有剩余商务座，有需要的旅客，请联系列车工作人员办理坐席升级手续，谢谢。

Ladies and gentlemen, there are still some business class seats available. Passengers who would like to upgrade their classes, please contact the attendants. Thank you.

- 女士们、先生们：欢迎乘坐复兴号列车。为了保持车内卫生，请将废弃物放进垃圾箱内。每个坐席背后的网袋内放置有清洁袋，请您将废弃物放进清洁袋内，由列车保洁员统一收取。餐车设在8号车厢，为您提供米饭套餐、酒水、饮料。祝您旅途愉快！

Ladies and gentlemen, welcome aboard the Fuxing train. To maintain a comfortable environment, please put the waste into the waste bin. A sanitary bag is provided and in the mash at the back of each seat. You can also leave trash in the sanitary bag. The cleaning crew will collect it during the trip. Carriage 8 is the dinning car, where we offer meals, wine, soft drinks and snacks. We wish you a pleasant journey.

6. 安全提示与文明乘车宣传

- 亲爱的旅客朋友们：欢迎乘坐和谐号列车，请根据您的车票号码对号入座，我们的列车员稍后将会进行检票。请您准备好车票和有效证件，感谢您的配合。

Dear passengers, welcome aboard the CRH train. Please be seated in the assigned seats according to the seat number on your tickets. Our train conductors will check your ticket soon. Please have your ticket and valid identification ready. Thank you for your cooperation.

- 各位旅客：请照看好您的小孩，不要让儿童在车厢内奔跑打闹、攀爬座椅、手扶门缝、触碰电茶炉，以免发生意外伤害，感谢配合。祝您旅途愉快！

Dear passengers, please take good care of your children, and do not let them run around or climb the seats. Please keep them away from the train doors and electronic boilers to avoid injuries. Thank you for your cooperation. Wish you a pleasant journey.

- 车厢提供自助开水，为保证安全，请依照指示，小心使用热水器。

Self-serviced hot water is available in every carriage. For safety reason, please read the instruction before using the water dispensers.

- 旅客们：欢迎乘车。您上车后，请核对车票，对号入座，并将随身携带的物品在行李架上放置稳妥。卧铺代散座车厢的旅客，请按照每个房间门口张贴的外层A、B、C标志对号入座。您的行李请放在行李架上或铺位底下。旅途中，请勿到上铺休息。请勿使用上铺卧具，请照看好您的孩子，不要让小孩到上铺玩耍，以免列车晃动时摔伤，谢谢配合。

Dear passengers, welcome aboard the train. Please sit in the assigned seat according to the seat number on your ticket and put your luggage safely on the luggage rack. In carts where seats are converted from berths, only the low berth seats are in use. Each berth is divided into three seats A, B and C as labeled. Luggage can be put on the luggage rack or underneath the low berth. The upper berth is not in use, so please do not lie down or sit there. Please take care of your children and do not let them play on the upper berth to avoid injuries. Thank you for your cooperation.

- 各位使用卧铺的旅客，请您看护好同行儿童，上下铺位时注意安全。

Please take good care of your children, especially when they climb up and down the sleepers.

- 为了使大家有一个舒适整洁的旅行环境，请大家爱护车厢内的设备。车座椅背后的小桌板是供大家放书刊、茶杯用的，沉重的东西请不要放在上面。途中也请大家不要趴在上面休息，以免损坏设备，影响使用。

To keep a tidy and comfortable traveling environment, please take care of the facilities in the train. The folding table in front of you is for holding books and drinks. To avoid injuries, please do not put heavy things or sleep on it.

• 旅客们：因列车空调故障，现在车内温度较高，列车将开启运行方向左侧部分车门。为确保安全，请大家不要靠近开启的车门或拥挤观望。

Dear passengers, the temperature inside the coach is high due to air conditioner malfunction. To lower the temperature, we are going to open some doors on the left side of the train. For your own safety, please keep away from the open doors.

• 旅客们：现在列车空调故障，乘务人员正在积极修复中，给您的旅行带来不便，敬请谅解，感谢配合。

Dear passengers, we are sorry for the discomfort caused by the air conditioner malfunction. The technician is repairing the air conditioner. Thank you for your patience and understanding.

• 持站票的旅客：由于出行旅客较多，为确保安全，请不要拥挤在车门口，更不要倚靠车门，给您带来的不便敬请谅解。

Passengers with standing tickets, please do not gather round or lean against the doors for your own safety. We're sorry for the discomfort caused by the heavy passenger flow.

• 车内所有范围，包括卫生间和进出口通道，一律严禁吸烟，谢谢合作。

Smoking is not allowed anywhere in the train including washing room and passenger way. Thank you for your cooperation.

• 女士们、先生们，列车上禁止携带危险物品。如果您已经带上车，请和列车工作人员联系，以便妥善处理。在每节车厢两端设有灭火器，车厢两端的第一个车窗为紧急窗口。列车上的红色按钮为紧急按钮，请勿随意触动。本次列车全程禁止吸烟，请勿在车厢任意部位吸烟。如有违反者，乘警将依据《铁路安全管理条例》进行处罚。

Ladies and gentlemen, poisonous and flammable articles are not allowed in the train. If you have any, please contact the attendants immediately. The extinguisher is available at the end of each carriage. The first window at the end of each carriage is the emergency exit. The red button can only be used in an emergency, and please do not touch it otherwise. Smoking is strictly prohibited during the whole trip. Violators will be punished according to the *Regulations on the Administration of Railway Safety*.

• 您在接打电话或互相交谈时，请勿大声喧哗，以免打扰其他旅客，感谢您的配合。

Please be respectful to other passengers by keeping your volume down while using mobile devices or talking to each other. Thank you.

• 列车发生紧急情况时，请听从列车工作人员安排。感谢您的关注，祝您旅途愉快！

In case of emergency, please follow the train attendants' instructions. Thanks for your attention. Have a nice trip.

• 女士们、先生们，列车已经到达：沈阳北站，感谢您乘坐动车组列车，再见。

Ladies and Gentlemen, the train has arrived at Shenyangbei Station. Thank you for taking our train. Hope to see you again.

- 旅客们，因车门集中调控系统故障，车门无法自动开启，需人工开启车门。请大家不要拥堵在通道和车门附近，乘务人员将逐个车厢开启车门。耽误您下车时间，请您谅解并予以配合。

Dear passengers, due to some mechanical issues of the central control system, the train doors will be opened manually. Please do not block the aisles or gather at the doors. The train attendants will open the door for you. We ask for your cooperation and understanding.

- 旅客们：大家好！我是本次列车的列车长，由于特殊原因，本次列车晚点。列车晚点给您带来诸多不便，我代表铁路运输企业向您表示诚挚的歉意！感谢您的理解和支持。

Dear passengers, I'm the chief of crew. The train will be delayed for some unexpected reasons. I apologize for all the inconvenience caused to you on behalf of the railway company. Thanks for your understanding.

- 各位旅客，请跟随车站工作人员自16站台南侧上扶梯到14站台登乘C2046次列车，到相同车厢座位号乘坐。。

Dear passengers, please follow our crew members and take the escalator in the south of platform 16. The escalator will lead you to the platform 14 and train C2046. Please take the seat with the same number as you have in the current trip.

- 各位旅客请注意，由于更换列车，持一等车厢的旅客请您到7号车厢对号入座。因此给您带来了不便，敬请谅解，多谢配合。

Dear passengers, attention please. Due to the change of trains, passengers in the first class carriage please go to carriage 7 and take the seat with the same number as you have on this train. We apologize for all the inconvenience. Thanks for your cooperation.

- 列车现因大雪晚点几分钟。我们正在努力赶点抢回耽误的时间。要在下一个车站下车特别是转乘的旅客，请整理好个人物品提前做好下车准备。请按照先后顺序下车。谢谢合作。

The train is delayed for a few minutes due to heavy snow. We will try to make up the lost time in the rest of the trip. Passengers who need to get off the train at the next station or transfer to another train, please get your luggage ready. Please get off the train in order. Thank you.

- 旅客朋友们请注意！列车上有名5岁的男孩跟家长走散了。小朋友身穿牛仔裤、绿色T恤，现在在餐车等候。请孩子的家长听到广播后，速到餐车。

Attention, please. A five-year old boy was found. The boy wears a pair of jeans and a green T-shirt. He is in the dining car now waiting for his parents.

- 现在是临时停车……分钟，请不要下车。

This is a temporary stop. The train will stay for... minutes. Please don't get off the train.

- 火车交通因大雾无法正常运行。

The train service is disrupted by heavy fog.

- 列车因大雪现在严重晚点。

The train is seriously delayed due to the heavy snow.

- 我们会给大家送去免费的面条和热茶。

We'll provide free noodles and hot tea to each passenger.

- 天气太热，我们将打开冷气，如果哪位旅客觉得不舒服，请告诉我们。

It is too hot. We will turn on the air conditioner. Please let us know if anyone doesn't feel well.

- 请别着急，列车将准时到达终点站。

Please don't worry, the train will be on time.

- 我们会努力抢回时间，列车很快就会正点。

We will try to make up the lost time. The train will soon be on schedule.

- D226次列车可以办理全额退款。

Full refund is available for train D226.

- 女士们、先生们：列车运行前方即将到达徐州东站。列车到站后将转换方向运行，您可踩下座椅外侧下部的旋转脚踏，轻轻推动座椅靠背旋转方向。旋转座椅时，请注意将自己的行李物品安放稳妥，防止损坏。

Ladies and gentlemen, we are arriving at Xuzhoudong Station. Our train will change the direction there. You may step down the rotation foot board on the outside under your seat, then gently push the seat back to rotate it. When doing so, please make sure your belongings are well placed to avoid any damage.

- 各位旅客，现在是临时停车。由于雷电，前方暂时没有开车信号，请在您的座位上跟我们一起耐心等候。因为是夜间休息时间，请大家保持安静，尽量不要到处走动，或者拥挤在车门前。

Dear passengers, this is a temporary stop. Due to the thunder, we could not get the green light signal ahead. Please wait patiently on your seat. It is rest time at night so please keep quiet. Please do not move around or gather near the gate.

- 旅客们：由于雪天站台地面湿滑，请您在下车时注意脚下安全。

Dear passengers, the platform is very slippery because of the snow. Please mind your steps while getting off the train.

- 列车即将到达虎门，下车时，请小心空隙并留意站台与车厢地面的高低差。

We will soon arrive at Humen Station, please be aware of the gap and difference in level between the train and the platform.

7. 临时停车

- 旅客们：现在是临时停车。

Dear passengers, this is a temporary stop.

8. 即将到站

- 旅客们：列车即将到达红安西站，到站时间17:05，停车3分钟。由于列车停站时间很短，未到站旅客请不要下车，感谢您的配合。

Dear passengers, the train will arrive at Honganxi Station at 17:05 and stay for 3 minutes. As the train will stay only for a short time, please do not get off the train if it isn't your destination. Thank you for your cooperation.

- 女士们、先生们：我们即将到达终点站上海虹桥站，请您整理好行李，准备下车。感谢您一路上给予的关心与支持，下次旅行再会。

Ladies and gentlemen, the train will arrive at Shanghaihongqiao Railway Station. Please take your belongings and be ready for exit. Thank you for your cooperation along the journey. We look forward to seeing you again.

• 女士们、先生们：列车前方停车站是西安北站，在本站下车的旅客，请提前做好准备。请勿倚靠在车门上，带小孩的旅客，请看管好自己的孩子。谢谢合作。

Ladies and gentlemen, the train is arriving at Xi'anbei Station, please get ready for arrival. Please do not lean on the door and take care of your children. Thanks for your cooperation.

• 请持有纸质车票的旅客，到站后按便捷换乘标志换乘接续列车。距离换乘地点最近的是10号车厢。

Passengers who hold paper tickets and need to change trains please follow the "Transfer" sign and go back to the station hall. The nearest transfer passage is next to coach 10.

Appendix II Basic Knowledge of Phonetics

1. 关于语音的几个概念

(1)字母：语言的书写形式。元音字母有a、e、i(y)、o、u。

(2)音标：词的语音形式。

(3)音素：音的最小的单位。英语中有48个音素。

(4)音节：由元音和辅音构成的发音单位。如：ap'ple、stu'dent、tea'cher、un'der'stand。

(5)元音：发音响亮，口腔中气流不受阻碍，是构成音节的主要音。英语中有20个元音。

(6)辅音：发音不响亮，口腔中气流受到阻碍，不是构成音节的主要音。英语中有28个辅音。

(7)开音节：①辅音+元音+辅音+e，如：name、bike；②辅音+元音，如：he、go、hi。

(8)闭音节：①辅音+元音+辅音，如：bad、bed、sit、hot、cup；②元音+辅音，如：it。

(9)重读音节：单词中发音特别响亮的音节。

2. 音标列表

国际音标（英语语音）

元音	单元音	前元音	[i:]	[i]	[e]	[æ]		
		中元音	[ʌ]	[ə:]	[ə]			
		后元音	[u:]	[u]	[ɔ:]	[ɔ]	[a:]	
	双元音	开合双元音	[ei]	[ai]	[ɔi]	[əu]	[au]	
		集中双元音	[iə]	[ɛə]	[uə]			
辅音	爆破音	清辅音	[p]	[t]	[k]			
		浊辅音	[b]	[d]	[g]			
	摩擦音	清辅音	[f]	[s]	[ʃ]	[θ]	[h]	
		浊辅音	[v]	[z]	[ʒ]	[ð]		
	破擦音	清辅音	[tʃ]	[tr]	[ts]			
		浊辅音	[dʒ]	[dr]	[dz]			
	鼻音	（浊辅音）	[m]	[n]	[ŋ]			
	舌则音	（浊辅音）	[l]	[r]				
	半元音	（浊辅音）	[w]	[j]				

注：①清音，即全体清辅音；浊音，即全体元音和全体辅音。

②[ŋ]又叫长鼻音或者后鼻音。

③半元音也属于辅音。

3. 英语常见语流现象：连读、加音、爆破、同化、省音、弱读、浊化

1) 连读

两个相邻单词首尾音素自然地拼读在一起，中间不停顿，被称为连读。连读只发生在同一意群之内，即意思联系紧密的短语或从句之内。

(1) 词尾辅音+词首元音，如：

Stand ͡ up.
Not ͡ at ͡ all.
Put ͡ it ͡ on, please.
Please pick ͡ it ͡ up.
It ͡ is ͡ an ͡ old book.
Let me have ͡ a look ͡ at ͡ it.
Ms Black worked in ͡ an ͡ office.
I called you half ͡ an ͡ hour ͡ ago.

(2) 词尾不发音r或re+词首元音，词尾r发音[r]，如：

Far ͡ away.
Here ͡ are four ͡ eggs.
Where ͡ is my cup?
Where ͡ are your brother ͡ and sister?
They're my father ͡ and mother.
I looked for ͡ it here ͡ and there.
There ͡ is a football under ͡ it.

注：当有意群需进行停顿时不可连读。如：

Is ͡ it a hat or ͡ a cat? (hat与or之间不可以连读)
There ͡ is ͡ a good book in my desk. (book与in之间不可以连读)
Can you speak ͡ English or French? (English与or之间不可以连读)
Shall we meet at ͡ eight or ten tomorrow morning? (meet与at，eight与or之间不可以连读)
She opened the door and walked ͡ in. (door与and之间不可以连读)

2) 加音

在连贯的语流中，人们往往会在两个元音之间加入一个外加音帮助发音，从而更加流畅地表达意思。

(1) 词尾元音[ʊ]/[u:]+词首元音，在词尾加上一个轻微的[w]。如：

Go w away.
How w and why did you come here?
The question is too w easy for him to answer.

(2) 词尾元音[ɪ]/[i:]+词首元音，在词尾加上一个轻微的[j]。如：

I j am Chinese.
She can't carry j it.
I j also need the j other one.
He j is very friendly to me.
She wants to study j English.
It'll take you three j hours to walk there.

3)失去爆破与不完全爆破

(1)失去爆破：爆破音+爆破音。

当两个爆破音[p]/[b]/[t]/[d]/[k]/[g]相邻时，前一个爆破音只按其发音部位做好发音口形、形成阻碍，而不爆破出来，稍微停顿后即发出后面的辅音。前一个爆破音被称为失去爆破。失去爆破的原因大体上是由于省力原则造成的。如：

Kept/Blackboard/Notebook/Goodbye/September/Suitcase.

Big boy.

Sharp pencil.

What time.

You must pay.

Ask Bob to sit behind me.

She took good care of the children.

(2)不完全爆破：

①爆破音+摩擦音。

爆破音[p]/[b]/[t]/[d]/[k]/[g]与摩擦音[f]/[v]/[s]/[z]/[ʃ]/[ʒ]/[θ]/[ð]/[r]/[h]相邻时，产生不完全爆破。发摩擦音时，发音器官并不形成阻碍而只形成一个很狭小的缝隙，让气流从缝隙中摩擦而出。如果一个爆破音与摩擦音相接，它爆破冲出的气流只能从狭小的缝隙中通过，这种爆破是不完全的。失去爆破的原因大体上是由于省力原则造成的。如：

Advance/Success.

A good view.

Old friends.

Just then.

Get through.

Make sure.

Night show.

Keep silence.

Keep that in mind.

②爆破音+破擦音。

爆破音与破擦音[tʃ]/[dʒ]/[tr]/[dr]相邻时，产生不完全爆破。如：

Picture/Object.

That child.

Good job.

Sweet dream.

Great changes.

A fast train.

③爆破音+鼻辅音。

爆破音与鼻辅音[m]/[n]/[ŋ]相邻时，在词中不完全爆破；在词尾鼻腔爆破。如：

Utmost/Admit/Midnight/Certain/Button/Garden.

Good morning.

Good night.

Start now.

I don't know.

Just moment.

A good neighbor.

④爆破音+边辅音。

爆破音与边辅音[l]相邻时,在词中不完全爆破;在词尾舌侧爆破。如:

Lately/Badly/Mostly/Friendly.

A bit louder.

I'd like to.

Straight line.

Good luck.

At last.

At lunch.

4)同化

人们在说话时往往会不自觉地让一个音受相邻音的影响,使它们变得与其相同或相似;或者两个音互相影响,变为第三个音。这两种现象被称为音的同化。同化可以发生在同一个词、复合词内或者句子相邻词之间。

(1)因声带的影响而发生的同化:

浊辅音可变为清辅音,如:of ([v]→[f]) course, his ([z]→[s]) pen, with ([ð]→[θ]) pleasure。

清辅音可变为浊辅音,如:like ([k]→[g]) that。

(2)因发音部位的影响而发生的同化:

①[t]+[j]→[tʃ],如:

Don't hurt yourself!

I'll let you go this time.

Don't you do that again.

It's very nice to meet you.

②[d]+[j]→[dʒ],如:

Did your sister come?

Would you please come in?

Could you read this for me please?

You didn't like English, did you?

③[s]+[j]→[ʃ],如:

I miss you.

May God bless you.

We will come this year.

④[z]+[j]→[ʒ],如:

Here's your ticket.

I love you because you are you.

Don't expect he tells you the truth.

5)省音

在快速、日常的言语中,一些音素被省略掉,被称为省音。省音能提高语速,使说话省力。在正式场合和语速慢的情况下,不是必须省音。

(1)同一单词内元音的省略,主要是非重读音节中的[ə]和[ɪ],如:ord(i)n(a)ry。

(2)当前一单词以辅音结尾,后一单词以[ə]开头时,[ə]常被省略,如:walk (a)way。

137

(3)当前一单词以否定形式-n't结尾，后一单词以辅音开头时，[t]常被忽略，如：
She isn'(t) there.
I didn'(t) hear you.
He can'(t) believe that.

(4)任何一个辅音，若后面紧跟着[h]，[h]可以不发音。如：
Come (h)ere!
Must (h)e [ti] go?
What will (h)e [wili] do?
Has (h)e done it before?
Tell (h)im to ask (h)er...

(5)将多个单词利用连读爆破等拼合在一起。如：
gotta (got to).
gonna (going to).
kinda (kind of).
lotsa (lots of).
gimme (give me).

6)强读式和弱读式
在一个句子中，有些词说得又轻又快，且较为含糊，而有些词则说得又重又慢，且较为清晰。那些说得响亮而清晰的词就是句子的重音所在。实词(包括名词、实义动词、形容词、副词、数词疑问词等)一般都接受句子重音，为重读词，采用强读式；虚词(包括介词、代词、连词、冠词、助动词、情态动词等功能词)一般都不接受句子重音，为非重读词，采用弱读式。

(1)一般规律：
①弱读式只出现在句子的非重读词中。如：Pass me[mɪ] the [ðə] book. 句中me、the弱读。
②单词单独出现或在句首或句尾时，都采用强读式。如：What are you listening to[tu:]?
③被特别强调的词，无论实词还是虚词都采用强读式。如：I am [æm] Peter. 我就是皮特。

(2)虚词弱读规律：
①长音变短音，如：she[ʃi:]弱读[ʃɪ]。
②元音前面的辅音被省略，如：him[hɪm]弱读[ɪm]。
③辅音前面的元音被省略，如：am[æm]弱读[m]。
④元音一般弱读为[ə]，如：can[kæn]弱读[kən]。
⑤部分虚词有多种弱读式，如：would[wʊd]弱读[əd]/[d]。

7)浊化
(1)[s]后面的清辅音要浊化。如：
①[k]浊化成[g]: scar/school/discussion。
②[t]浊化成[d]: stand/student/mistake。
③[p]浊化成[b]: spring/spirit/expression。

(2)美音中，当[t]出现在两个元音之间并且处于非重读位置的时候，[t]需要浊化成一个近似于[d]的音。这样，writer听起来和rider的发音几乎没有区别。如：
Letter/water/better/duty/bitter/cit.

I got it.

Would you please pick it up?

注：[t]如果处于重读位置的话，即使在两个元音之间也不需要浊化。请比较：

清晰的[t]	浊化的[t]
I'talian	'Italy
a'tomic	'atom
La'tino	'Latin
pho'tographer	'photograph

(3)美音中，当[t]前面是一个元音，后面是一个模糊的[l]，且处于非重读位置，[t]也需要浊化成一个近似于[d]的音。如：

Battle/bottle/cattle/little/rattle/settle.

(4)美音中，当[t]前面是一个清辅音或前鼻音[n]，后面是一个元音，且处于非重读位置，[t]也需要浊化成一个近似于[d]的音，如：

Twenty/fifty/center/after/faster/actor/sister.

Appendix III   Railway Service Rules

1. According to the relevant provisions of Contract Law, children are not allowed to take the train alone in principle. They have to be accompanied by adults with full capacity for civil conduct.

依据合同法有关规定，儿童原则上不能单独乘车，须与具备完全民事行为能力的成年人同行。

2. An adult passenger can be accompanied by one child under 1.2 meters in height, free of charge. If there are more than one child under 1.2 meters, only one of them is free of ticket, while the others shall purchase child tickets. Children between 1.2 to 1.5 meters high shall purchase child tickets; those higher than 1.5 meters shall purchase full-price seat tickets.

Children are allowed (for free, or with charges according to the provisions above) to share berths with adult passengers who have purchased sleeping berth tickets.

一名成年人旅客可以免费携带一名身高不足1.2m的儿童。如果身高不足1.2m的儿童超过一名时，一名儿童免费，其他儿童请购买儿童票。儿童身高为1.2~1.5m的，请购买儿童票；超过1.5m的，请购买全价座票。

成年人旅客持卧铺车票时，儿童可以与其共用一个卧铺，并按上述规定免费或购票。

3. When purchasing child tickets on 12306.cn, you can add children's valid IDs to My Passengers and buy children's tickets for them. For children who don't have valid IDs, the ID document of an accompanying adult (the name, ID type, and ID number should belong to the same person) could be used to purchase child tickets.

在12306.cn网站购买儿童票时，儿童有有效身份证件的，可添加为乘车人，儿童没有有效身份证件的，可以使用同行成年人身份信息(姓名、证件类型、证件号码均为同一成年人)购票。

4. Child tickets are available for seat tickets, extra fast tickets, and air-conditioned tickets at a discount of 50% of the total of seat tickets and other published subsidiary tickets. Children getting on board for free or with child tickets will have to purchase full-price berth tickets if they use the berth all alone, as well as a half-price air-conditioned ticket if the train is air-conditioned. The seat type of a child ticket shall be the same as that of the accompanying adults' ticket, and the destination cannot be farther than that of the adult's ticket.

儿童票可享受客票、加快票和空调票的优惠，儿童票票价按相应客票和附加票公布票价的50%计算。免费乘车及持儿童票乘车的儿童单独使用卧铺时，另收全价卧铺票价，有空调时还另收半价空调票票价。儿童票的座别与成年人旅客的车票相同，到站不能远于成年人旅客车票的到站。

5. In some large stations, there are service counters providing priority service on ticket purchase, entering the station, boarding, luggage check-in and so on for the elderly, infants

and children, the sick, the disabled and pregnant passengers. Some stations also provide wheelchair services for people with disabilities. Please consult the station for details.

部分较大站设有服务台，为老、幼、病、残、孕旅客提供优先购票、优先进站、优先乘车、优先托办行李等服务，有的车站还可为行动不便的残疾人旅客提供轮椅服务。详情请咨询乘车站。

6. The maximum limit of free cabin luggage for each passenger are: 10 kg for children (including those free of tickets), 35 kg for diplomats and 20 kg for other passengers. The maximum dimension of each item is 160 cm in total (rod-shaped items 200 cm) for traditional trains, and 130 cm for EMU trains; the maximum weight for each item is 20 kg. Foldable wheelchairs used by people with disabilities are not included in the above range.

每名旅客免费携带物品的重量和体积是：儿童(含免费乘车的儿童)10kg，外交人员35kg，其他旅客20kg。每件物品外部尺寸长、宽、高之和不超过160cm，杆状物品不超过200cm，但乘坐动车组列车不超过130cm；重量不超过20kg。残疾人代步所用的折叠式轮椅不计入上述范围。

7. Announcement on items prohibited or restricted in a train or train station:

In accordance with *Railway Safety Management Regulations* issued by the State Council as well as other state laws, administrative regulations, and rules concerned, the items prohibited or restricted to take on board a train or to a train station are listed as follows in an effort to maintain public security and travel safety for all:

(1) Guns and bullets (key components included):

Guns for military use (pistols, rifles, submachine guns, machine guns, and riot guns) and their bullets (blank bullet, combat bullet, test bullet, and instructor bullet); guns for civilian use (air gun, hunting gun, sport gun, and anesthetic gun) and their bullets; guns for other purposes (prop gun, imitation gun, starting gun, steel ball gun, fire extinguisher gun); as well as the prototype or replica of the above-mentioned items.

For military personnel, armed police, public security officers, militia personnel, shooting athletes, and other passengers who have to travel with guns and/or bullets, applicable laws and regulations of China shall be followed. Relevant management rules such as keeping the guns and bullets separately shall be strictly observed.

(2) Explosives:

Bomb, flare, incendiary bomb, smoke bomb, signal bomb, tear bomb, gas bomb, hand grenade, and other ammunitions; explosive, detonator, detonating fuse and cord, blasting agent, exploder, and other blasting equipment; all kinds of firework and firecrackers, black powder, pyrotechnic powder, fuse and other pyrotechnic products; as well as the replica of the above-mentioned items.

(3) Instruments:

Dagger, three-edged knife (that for machine processing included), switchblade with the self-locking device and other restricted singles- and double-edge knives; kitchen knife, table knife, butcher knife, axe and other restricted sharp or blunt objects that may endanger the safety of other passengers; baton, tear gun (and other items alike), taser (and other items alike), nail gun, items for self-defense, bow, crossbow and other items of similar nature.

(4) Inflammable and explosive items:

Hydrogen, methane, ethane, butane, natural gas, ethylene, propylene, acetylene (soluble in medium), carbon monoxide, liquefied petroleum gas, Freon, oxygen (oxygen bags for medical purpose excluded), water gas and other compressed and liquefied gas; gasoline, kerosene, diesel oil, benzene, ethanol (alcohol), acetone, ether, paints, thinners, turpentine oil and other liquid with flammable solvent or flammable liquid; red phosphorus, flash powder, solid alcohol, celluloid, foaming agent H and other flammable solid; yellow phosphorus, white phosphorus, nitrocellulose (film included), oil-paper and other spontaneously ignited items; metal potassium, sodium, lithium, calcium carbide, magnesium aluminum powder and other water-reactive chemicals; potassium permanganate, potassium chlorate, sodium peroxide, potassium peroxide, lead peroxide, peracetic acid, hydrogen peroxide and other oxidants and organic peroxides.

(5) Hypertoxic, corrosive, radioactive, infectious, and dangerous items:

Highly toxic chemicals (cyanide, arsenic, selenium powder, and phenol alike) and farm chemicals (tetramine, raticide, and pesticide included); sulfuric acid, hydrochloric acid, nitric acid, sodium hydroxide, potassium hydroxide, storage battery (with potassium hydroxide solid, acid or alkali liquid alike), mercury and other corrosive items; radioisotopes and other radioactive materials; pathogens of hepatitis B virus, Bacillus anthracis, Bacillus tuberculosis, HIV and other infectious diseases; other dangerous objects listed in the *List of Dangerous Goods for Railway Transport* and those of unidentified nature that might be dangerous.

(6) Items that endanger railway safety or public health:

Strong magnetized objects that may undermine railway signal, items with strong and irritating smell, foul-smelling objects, live animals (guide dog excluded), objects that dampen public health, and those that damage or pollute railway station, train facilities, equipment, parts or components.

(7) Only a limited amount of the following items is allowed: no more than 20 mL of nail polish, delustering, and hair dye; no more than 120 mL of perm lotion, mousse, hair spray, pesticide, air freshener, and other pressing spray bottles; two small boxes of safety matches; two lighters.

(8) Applicable Chinese laws, administrative regulations, and rules shall be followed in the handling of other prohibited and restricted items.

(9) In case of violation, the relevant law and regulations of China shall be followed.

铁路进站乘车禁止和限制携带物品的公告：

根据国务院颁布的《铁路安全管理条例》等国家法律、行政法规、规章等规定，为维护铁路公共安全，确保广大旅客安全旅行，现将铁路进站乘车禁止和限制携带物品公布如下：

(1)请勿携带以下枪支、子弹类(含主要零部件)：手枪、步枪、冲锋枪、机枪、防暴枪等军用枪以及各类配用子弹(含空包弹、战斗弹、检验弹、教练弹)；气枪、猎枪、运动枪、麻醉注射枪等民用枪以及各类配用子弹；道具枪、仿真枪、发令枪、钢珠枪、消防灭火枪等其他枪支；上述物品的样品、仿制品。

军人、武警、公安人员、民兵、射击运动员等人员携带枪支子弹的，按照国家法律法规有关规定办理，并严格执行枪弹分离等有关枪支管理规定。

(2)请勿携带以下爆炸物品类：炸弹、照明弹、燃烧弹、烟幕弹、信号弹、催泪弹、毒气弹、手榴弹等弹药；炸药、雷管、导火索、导爆索、爆破剂、发爆器等爆破器材；礼花弹、烟花、鞭炮、摔炮、拉炮、砸炮、发令纸等各类烟花爆竹以及黑火药、烟火药、引火线等烟火制品；上述物品的仿制品。

(3)请勿携带以下器具：匕首、三棱刀(包括机械加工用的三棱刮刀)、带有自锁装置的弹簧刀以及其他类似的单刃、双刃刀等管制刀具；管制刀具以外的，可能危及旅客人身安全的菜刀、餐刀、屠宰刀、斧子等利器、钝器；警棍、催泪器、催泪枪、电击器、电击枪、射钉枪、防卫器、弓、弩等其他器具。

(4)请勿携带以下易燃易爆物品：氢气、甲烷、乙烷、丁烷、天然气、乙烯、丙烯、乙炔(溶于介质的)、一氧化碳、液化石油气、氟利昂、氧气(供病人吸氧的袋装医用氧气除外)、水煤气等压缩气体和液化气体；汽油、煤油、柴油、苯、乙醇(酒精)、丙酮、乙醚、油漆、稀料、松香油及含易燃溶剂的制品等易燃液体；红磷、闪光粉、固体酒精、赛璐珞、发泡剂H等易燃固体；黄磷、白磷、硝化纤维(含胶片)、油纸及其制品等自燃物品；金属钾、钠、锂、碳化钙(电石)、镁铝粉等遇湿易燃物品；高锰酸钾、氯酸钾、过氧化钠、过氧化钾、过氧化铅、过氧乙酸、过氧化氢等氧化剂和有机过氧化物。

(5)请勿携带以下剧毒性、腐蚀性、放射性、传染性、危险性物品：氰化物、砒霜、硒粉、苯酚等剧毒化学品以及毒鼠强等剧毒农药(含灭鼠药、杀虫药)；硫酸、盐酸、硝酸、氢氧化钠、氢氧化钾、蓄电池(含氢氧化钾固体、注有酸液或碱液的)、汞(水银)等腐蚀性物品；放射性同位素等放射性物品；乙肝病毒、炭疽杆菌、结核杆菌、艾滋病病毒等传染病病原体；《铁路危险货物品名表》所列除上述物品以外的其他危险物品以及不能判明性质可能具有危险性的物品。

(6)请勿携带以下危害列车运行安全或公共卫生的物品：可能干扰列车信号的强磁化物，有强烈刺激性气味的物品，有恶臭等异味的物品，活动物(导盲犬除外)，可能妨碍公共卫生的物品，能够损坏或者污染车站、列车服务设施、设备、备品的物品。

(7)限量携带以下物品：不超过20mL的指甲油、去光剂、染发剂；不超过120mL的冷烫精、摩丝、发胶、杀虫剂、空气清新剂等自喷压力容器；安全火柴2小盒；普通打火机2个。

(8)其他禁止和限制旅客携带物品按照国家法律、行政法规、规章规定办理。

(9)违规携带上述物品，依照国家相关法律法规的规定处理。

8. The ticket counter, station entrance, ticket gate, and platforms are a few minutes' walks away. For passenger safety and station order, ticket sales and check will be halted before train departure; please refer to the station announcement for the time ahead. Please reserve enough time to get your ticket and get ready to board the train. Take the valid ID document used for purchasing the ticket with you for your convenience.

There might be a queue at the ticket window, security check, ID verification counter, ticket gate, and luggage consignment counter. Please reserve enough time for your convenience.

Please pay attention to the station announcement, display, staff reminder of train platform, waiting room, check-in gate, ticket check time, train departure time and other important information.

车站售票厅、进站口、检票口、站台之间有一定距离，需要一定的行走时间，为了确保旅客人身安全和铁路运输秩序，车站将在开车时间之间提前停止售票、检票，请关注车站关于提前停止售票、检票时间的公告。请在停止售票、检票时间前抵达车站办理购票、候车，同时准备好购票时所使用的乘车人有效身份证件原件，避免耽误乘车。

车站售票窗口、安检口、实名制验证口、检票口、行包托运受理窗口排队人数可能较多，请预留足够的时间办理购票、行李托运、安全检查、实名制验证、检票等。

进站、候车时，请注意广播、电子显示屏、工作人员等关于列车停靠站台、候车室、检票口、开始检票时间、开车时间等信息提示。

9. According to relevant laws and regulations, all passengers and their belongings carried are subject to security check. When entering the station, please place your luggage and belongings in the dangerous goods inspector and pass through the security gate. If you are traveling with a guide dog, please wait for an inspection with your dog.

There might be a queue at the security check, so please reserve enough time.

依据国家有关法律法规规定，所有旅客及随身携带物品都必须经过安全检查。进站乘车时，请将携带物品放入危险品检查仪、通过安检门接受安全检查，请予配合。

视力残疾旅客携带导盲犬进站时，请携带导盲犬接受安全检查。

车站安检口可能排队人数较多，请预留足够的时间到达车站。

10. Passenger can board the designated train from any intermediate station covered by the purchased journey on the date of travel, but the untraveled section of the journey will not be refunded.

按照车票票面指定的日期、车次，乘客可以在中途站上车，但未乘区间的票价不予退还。

11. Passengers shall go through the following procedures in case they lost the ID document used in ticket purchase:

(1) In cases the passenger lost the ID document before boarding, he/she shall apply for an ID certificate (provisional railway ID certificate included) from a competent issuing authority of the lost ID document and then board the train with the certificate.

(2) In cases the passenger lost the ID document on the train or before exiting the station, he/she shall apply for a replacement ticket and pay a service fee. An electronic train-riding record (or a paper one in special cases) will be issued if the seat is verified to be occupied normally on the train; or a paper record will be issued if the station has confirmed that the ticket purchased with the lost ID has not been used for exit. Within 30 days from the date of travel, the passenger shall take the ID certificate issued by a competent issuing authority of the lost ID document and the replaced ticket (and the paper train-riding record, if any) to the refund counters at any intermediate stations to apply for a refund of the fare charged repeatedly for the journey covered in both the original and the replaced tickets. In cases where a station exit record is identified for the lost ID, the replaced ticket shall not be refunded. Otherwise, the service fee for ticket refund shall be exempted, but the fee charged beforehand will not be refunded.

旅客购票后，丢失购票身份证件的，按以下方式处理。

(1)旅客在乘车前丢失证件的，应到该有效身份证件的发证机构办理身份证明(含铁路临时身份乘车证明)，凭身份证明进出站乘车。

(2)旅客在列车上、出站前丢失证件的，须先办理补票手续并按规定支付手续费，列车核验席位使用正常的，开具电子客运记录(特殊情况可开具纸质客运记录)；车站核验车票无出站检票记录的，开具纸质客运记录。旅客应在乘车日期之日起30

日内，凭该有效身份证件发证机构办理的身份证明和后补车票(如开具纸质客运记录，还应携带纸质客运记录)，到列车的经停站退票窗口办理后补车票与原票乘车区间一致部分的退票手续。办理退票手续时，如核查丢失证件有出站记录的，后补车票不予退票；无出站记录的，办理退票时，不收退票费，已核收的手续费不予退还。

12. Smoking is strictly prohibited anywhere on EMU trains, or in the coaches of conventional trains. Passengers can find smoking areas by the door or in the vestibule on a limited number of conventional trains.

动车组列车全程各部位严禁吸烟。普通旅客列车车厢内严禁吸烟，目前部分列车在车门或车厢连接处设有吸烟点。

13. Endorsement refers to the procedures to take when passengers change the date of travel, train number, or seat (berth). The railway department reminds passengers that endorsement can only be handled when there is enough capacity (i.e., available tickets). Only the date of travel, train number, or seat (berth) can be changed, and the departure station and arrival station (except for stations in the same city) can not be changed.

改签是指旅客变更乘车日期、车次、席(铺)位时需办理的签证手续。铁路部门提醒旅客，改签以铁路有运输能力(即可售车票)为前提，只可变更乘车日期、车次、席(铺)位，不可变更发站和到站(同城车站除外)。

14. Since June 10, 2015, the railway passenger transport department launched the "change of destination" service, i.e. after purchasing tickets, passengers can, based on the change of their travel itinerary, choose a new destination and travel by another train available within the presale period with a different departure date, train number or seat.

自2015年6月10日起，在铁路客运部门推出"变更到站"服务，即：旅客购票后，可根据行程变化，重新选择新的目的地，在车票预售期内变更到站及乘车日期、车次、席位。

15. More than 48 hours (not included) before the train departure time, you can endorse your ticket to that of another train available within the pre-sale period. Within 48 hours before the train departure time, you can endorse your ticket to travel by another train scheduled to depart before the original train, or after the original train but before 24:00 of the date of departure of the original train; it is not possible to endorse the ticket to a train scheduled to depart the next day or later. After the train has departed, passenger can still get the ticket endorsed to another train scheduled to depart on the same date, but only at the departure station of the original ticket, and the endorsed ticket cannot be refunded.

在有运输能力的前提下，开车前48小时(不含)以上，可改签预售期内的其他列车。开车前48小时以内，可改签开车前的其他列车，也可改签开车后至票面日期当日24:00之间的其他列车，不办理票面日期次日及以后的改签。开车之后，旅客仍可改签当日其他列车。但已经办理"变更到站"的车票，不再办理改签。改签车票不予退票。

16. Please go to a station ticket counter for the reimbursement receipt of the refund service fee within 180 days since the endorsement or change of destination through 12306.cn, with the passenger's valid ID document used to purchase the ticket.

请在12306.cn网站办理退票或变更到站之日起180日内，凭购票时所使用的乘车人有效身份证件原件到车站售票窗口索取退票费报销凭证。

17. If the passenger is unable to take a train as per the departure date, train number, seat or berth described on the ticket due to railway responsibility, staff in the station or on the train will provide proper arrangements. If the rearranged train, seat, or berth costs more than the original one, the excess part of the fare will not be charged; otherwise, the fare difference will be refunded at the departure or destination station, and no refund service fee will be charged.

因铁路责任使旅客不能按票面记载的日期、车次、座别、卧别乘车时，车站或列车乘务人员将重新妥善安排。重新安排的列车、座席、铺位高于原车票等级的，超过部分票价不予补收；低于原车票的，由乘车站或到站退还票价差额，不收退票费。

18. No refund service fee is charged if the ticket is refunded more than 8 days (including) before the departure date; 5% of the ticket price is charged if the ticket is refunded more than 48 hours before the train departure; 10% is charged if less than 48 hours and more than 24 hours; and 20% is charged if less than 24 hours.

If the ticket is endorsed or if the destination station of the ticket is changed between 48 hours to 8 days before the train departure time, to another train scheduled to depart at least 8 days later, 5% refund fee shall be charged for the endorsed/changed ticket even if the ticket is refunded at least 8 days before train departure.

If the price of the new ticket after endorsement or change of destination is lower than that of the original one, the difference will be refunded after a refund service fee is charged to the price difference as per the existing refund service fee rules.

The refund fee shall be rounded up to RMB 0.5, with the value less than RMB 0.25 rounded off, that more than RMB 0.25 and less than RMB 0.75 taken as RMB 0.5, and the value more than RMB 0.75 rounded to RMB 1. The minimum refund fee is RMB 2.

开车前8天(含)以上退票的，不收取退票费；票面乘车站开车时间前48小时以上退票的，按票价5%计退票费；24小时以上、不足48小时退票的，按票价10%计退票费，不足24小时退票的，按票价20%计退票费。

开车前48小时~8天期间内，改签或变更到站至距开车8天以上的其他列车，又在距开车8天前退票的，仍核收5%的退票费。

办理车票改签或"变更到站"时，新车票票价低于原车票的，退还差额，对差额部分核收退票费并执行现行退票费标准。

上述计算的尾数以0.5元为单位，尾数小于0.25元的舍去，0.25元及以上且小于0.75元的计为0.5元，0.75元及以上的进为1元。退票费最低按2元计收。

19. Endorsement or change of destination station is available to one ticket for only one time. The service of changing destination station is not available for endorsed tickets and tickets whose destination station has been changed cannot be endorsed. If the passenger cancels the trip after endorsement or change of destination, he can get a refund according to refund rules. Endorsed tickets cannot be refunded after train departure.

一张车票可以办理一次改签。对已改签车票暂不提供"变更到站"服务，已"变更到站"的车票也不可办理改签。车票改签后，旅客取消旅行的，可以按规定退票，但开车后改签的车票不能退票。

20. In the case that the original ticket is purchased by cash, if the price of the new ticket after endorsement or change of destination is higher than that of the original one, the difference will be charged; otherwise, the difference will be refunded after a refund service

fee is charged to the price difference as per the existing refund service fee rules (all in cash).

In the case that the original ticket is purchased at the ticket window by a bank card or on the 12306.cn website by online payment means, the passenger has to pay the full price of the new ticket after endorsement or change of destination with a bank card if the price of the new ticket is higher than that of the original ticket, and the refund of the original ticket will be returned within the prescribed time to the bank card or online payment account used to purchase the ticket; otherwise, the difference will be refunded within the prescribed time to the bank card or online payment account used to purchase the ticket after a refund service fee is charged to the price difference as per the existing refund service fee rules.

原车票使用现金购票的，当改签或"变更到站"后的新车票票价高于原车票时，补收差额；当新车票票价低于原车票时，退还差额，并对差额部分核收退票费并执行现行退票费标准(均为现金)。

原车票在铁路售票窗口使用银行卡购票，或者在12306.cn网站使用在线支付工具购票的，按发卡银行或在线支付工具相关规定，当改签或"变更到站"后的新车票票价高于原车票时，应使用银行卡支付新车票全额票款，原车票票款在规定时间退回原购票时所使用的银行卡或在线支付工具；当新车票票价低于原车票时，退还差额，对差额部分核收退票费并执行现行退票费标准，应退票款在规定时间退回原购票时所使用的银行卡或在线支付工具。

Appendix IV: Terms of High-speed Railway both in Chinese and in English

高速铁路客运服务英语

High-speed Railway	高铁
Hexie Hao (CRH series EMU)	和谐号
Fuxing Hao (CR series)	复兴号
Vibrant Express (MTR)	动感号
Z—Non-Stop Express	直达
T—Express	特快
K—Fast	快速
General Fast Train	普通旅客快车
General Train	普通旅客列车
Temporary	临时
Temporary Tourist Train	临时旅游列车
Suburban Commuter Rail	市郊铁路线
Steam Train	蒸汽火车
Bullet Trains	动车
Normal Trains/Regular Trains	普通列车
Green Trains	绿皮火车
First Class Seat	一等座
Second Class Seat	二等座
Business Class Seat	商务座
Standing Ticket	无座票
Soft Sleeper	软卧
Hard Sleeper	硬卧
Bullet Train Sleeper	动卧
Deluxe Soft Sleeper	高级软卧
High-speed Railway Stations	高铁站
The Departure Station	出发站
The Arrival Station	到达站
The High-speed Railway Network	高速铁路网络
Intercity Railway	城际铁路
Short-distance Intercity High-speed Trains	短距离城际高速列车

Real-name Purchasing System	实名购票系统
Replacement Ticket	补票
Ticket Scalping	倒票
Double-decker Bullet Train	双层动车
Public Transport	公共交通工具
High-speed Maglev Train	高速磁悬浮列车
Maglev Technologies	磁悬浮技术
The Automatic Train	自动列车
Mileage of Operational Railway	铁路运营里程
Rail Transportation	铁路运输
The Transportation System	运输系统
Railway Authorities	铁路部门
High-speed Train Trip	高铁旅游
Tourism Services	旅游服务
The Top 10 Hottest Destinations	十大热门旅游地
An Economic Belt	经济带
A Country with Strong Transportation Network	交通强国
Affordable Price	合理的价格
Communal Plugs	公共插头
Private Compartment	私人隔间
Intelligent Robots	智能机器人
The Flexible Pricing Mechanism	灵活的定价机制
Non-rush Periods	非高峰期
Preferential Prices	优惠价格
China Railway Express	中铁快运
Railway Transportation Sectors	铁路运输部门
Run Chart	运行图
Trial Operation/Run	试运行
Intercity High-speed Railway	城际高铁
Dedicated Rail Link	铁路专线
Speed Cut	减速
Test Period	测试期间
Technical Reliability	技术可靠性
Dual-speed System	双速制
Staggered Parking Track	交错停车

Appendix IV

149

Rolling Stock	轨道车辆
Track Maintenance Worker	养路工
Protective Fence	防护栏
Passenger Flow	客流量
Standard Seat	普通座
Derailment Coefficient	脱轨系数
Trial Price	试行运价
Gapless Rail	无缝钢轨
Ballastless Track	无碴轨道
On-schedule Rate	正点率
Train Set with Power Car	动车组
Vehicle Type	车型
Passenger Rail Transport	铁路客运
Track Gauge	轨距
At-grade Crossings	铁道交叉口
Conventional High-speed Railway	常规高速铁路
High-speed Railway Malfunction	高铁故障
The High-speed Railway Malfunction Created Gigantic Passenger Backups	高铁故障造成大量旅客滞留

Appendix V Abbreviations for High-speed Railway

CARS	the China Academy of Railway Sciences	中国铁道科学研究院集团有限公司
CEMU	China-standard Electric Multiple Units	中国标准电动动车组
CDRC	the China Railway Design Corporation	中国铁路设计总公司
CR	China State Railway Group Co., Ltd.	中国国家铁路集团有限公司
CRRC	CRRC Corporation Limited	中国中车股份有限公司
CTCS	Chinese Train Control Systems	中国列车控制系统
HSR	high-speed railway	高速铁路
ISO	International Organization for Standardization	国际标准化组织
MU	Multiple Units	动车组
NDRC	the National Development and Reform Commission	国家发展和改革委员会
OBOR	the Belt and Road Initiative	"一带一路"倡议
REB	the Railroad Economic Belt	铁路经济带
NRA	National Railway Administration of the People's Republic of China	中国国家铁路局
CREC	China Railway Group Limited	中国中铁股份有限公司

Service Expressions for Foreigners

1. How to Take the Train

• Excuse me, where can I take the bus/metro/subway to the train station? (Show your ticket or the Chinese name of the station.)

请问去火车站的公车/地铁在哪里乘坐?

• Please take me to the train station, thanks! (Show your ticket or Chinese name of the station to taxi driver.)

请带我去火车站,谢谢!

• Please drive me to this train station. (Show the Chinese name of the station to the taxi driver.)

请送我到这个火车站。

• Excuse me, is there a shuttle bus to the train station? (at an airport)

请问有去火车站的机场大巴吗?

• How long will it take to go to the train station from here? /How long will it take to this train station?

从这里到火车站需要多久?

• Would you please tell me when we arrive at the train station? Thank you! (asking when you are on a bus or subway to the train station)

到这个火车站的时候,麻烦你提醒我下车,谢谢!

• Excuse me. Where is this train station?

请问这个火车站在哪里?

2. At the Train Station

• Where is the ticket office, please?

请问售票厅在哪里?

• I have made a booking online, where can I collect my tickets?

我在网上订了票,请问我在哪里可以取票?

• Where can I collect my train ticket booked online?

网络订票的取票窗口在哪里?

• This is my pick up number and passport. I need to collect the ticket. (at the ticket-collecting counter)

这是我的订票号和护照,请你帮我把票取出来。

• A second class seat ticket from Shanghai to Beijing on train G6 on March 12th, please.

请帮我买一张3月12号G6次上海到北京的二等座。

• I missed my train, is it possible to change my ticket for a later train?

我错过了火车,我能改签吗?

- Hello! I would like to pick up my ticket. This is my ticket pickup number and passport.

你好！我要取票，这是我的订单号和护照。

- Which window is for changing ticket?

请问改签窗口在哪里？

- Which window is for ticket refunds?

请问哪个是退票窗口？

- Excuse me, I need to change my ticket(s) to (train number and date), please.

你好，请帮我改签到……车次。

- I missed my train. Can I change my ticket for a later train?

我误车了，能改签下一车吗？

- Where is the waiting room for my train, please? (show your ticket)

请问我在哪个候车厅候车？

- Could you please tell me which boarding gate is for my train? (Show your ticket to the staff.)

请问我在哪个检票口检票？

- Excuse me, could you tell me where the restroom is?

你好，请问卫生间在哪里？

- Will you please help me find a red hat porter?

你能帮我找个小红帽(行李员)吗？

- Excuse me. Where is the entrance to the railway station?

请问进站口在哪里？

- Could you please tell me where I should wait for my train? (show your ticket)

请问我应该去那个候车室？

- Waiting for Boarding.

正在候车。

- Could you please tell me which boarding gate I should go to for this ticket? (show your ticket)

请问我应该哪个检票口检票？

- Ticket Checking.

正在检票。

- Could you tell me which platform I should go to? (show your ticket)

请问我应该在哪个站台上车？

- Could you please help me find a luggage porter?

你能帮我找个行李员吗？

- Where is the Information Desk?

请问问讯处在哪里？

- Where is the bathroom?

请问洗手间在哪里？

- Excuse me, when is the boarding time?

请问登车时间是多少？

- Do you know where is the ticket checking window? / Where is the boarding gate?

你知道检票口是哪一个吗？

153

- The train's running late. What time is the next train?

火车晚点了。下一班火车什么时候开？

- The train's been canceled. What time is the last train?

火车被取消了。最后一班列车是什么时候？

- Where do I change for Dalian?

我要在哪里换乘去大连的车？

- I'd like a soft sleeper from Beijing to Shanghai.

我要一张从北京到上海的软卧。

3. On the Train

- Is this the right platform for Beijing?

这是去北京的站台吗？

- Excuse me. Could you tell me which coach I should board? (show your ticket)

请问我从哪个车厢上车？

- Where is my seat/berth, please? (show your ticket)

请问我的座位/铺位在哪里？

- Excuse me, my companion(s) and I are in separated seats, would you mind exchanging seats/berth with us?

对不起，我和我的同伴座位不在一起，请问你是否愿意和我们换一下座位/铺位？

- Where is the dining car, please?

请问餐车在哪里？

- Would you please tell me where I can find the train conductor please? (for those who lost their tickets after boarding)

我的车票弄丢了，请问去哪里可以找到列车长？

- Where should I go to report a lost ticket?

请问去哪里补票？

- May I ask if the train is delayed, and when it will reach my destination (show your ticket)?

请问火车有晚点吗？什么时候到我的目的地？

- Will you please inform me 10 minutes before my arrival, thanks a lot!

请在到站前10分钟提醒我准备下车，谢谢！

4. After the Journey

- Where is the exit, please?

请问出站口在哪里？

- I have to transit here; which way should I go, please?(show your ticket)

我要转火车，请问我应该怎么走？

- Excuse me, where could I deposit my luggage?

请问我可以在哪里寄存行李？

- Excuse me, is there a shuttle bus to the airport please?

请问这里有去机场的大巴吗？

- Where do I go for the bus station/subway station, please?

请问公车站/地铁站怎么走？

- Where can I take a taxi?

在哪里能打出租？

- Where can I take the subway?

请问地铁入口在哪里?

- Where is the bus station?

请问公交站在哪里?

- Where is the left-luggage office?

哪里可以寄存行李?

Service Expressions for Train Crew Members

1.Train Ticket Service Expressions

- Which ticket do you want?

您想买哪张票?

- When will you leave?/When do you want your ticket?

您要买什么时间的票?

- There is a ticket (available) at/around six./There are three tickets at/around six.

(大概)六点钟有一张(三张)票。

- Sorry, there are no tickets available to Hangzhou.

抱歉,没有开往杭州的火车票。

- Sorry, tickets from Harbin to Jilin are sold out.

抱歉,哈尔滨到吉林的火车票已售完。

- Would you take others(tickets)?/Would you like others?/How about others?

其他票可以吗?

- Please show me your student's ID card/Citizen Identity Card.

请出示您的学生证/身份证。

- Platform tickets are not available for CRH trains.

高铁列车不售站台票。

- Please double check tickets and change before leaving.

请当面确认票款。

- Passengers could change their tickets free only once.

旅客只能免费改签一次车票。

- Only today's tickets for train G907 are available. Standard fare is RMB 83.

只售今日G907次,全价车票83元。

- Entry-exit formalities shall be stopped 20 minutes before train departs.

开车前20分钟停止办理出入境手续。

- I am sorry to say that you have brought tickets at prices in category two. So you will make up the price difference between category one and two.

对不起,您的车票是二等票,需要补交一、二等票价的差额。

- You can only bring with you one child under 1.2 meters free of charge. So you should buy a Children ticket for the other.

您只能免费携带一名身高不够1.2m的儿童,所以另一位要补儿童票。

- Please add more 11 yuan for your over journey. Have you got change?

您越站乘车,需要加补11元钱,您有零钱吗?

- You may take your baby free of charge.

您可以免费带你的小孩乘车。

- An adult passenger can take with him one child (who is) under 1.2 meters in height free of charge.

  每一位成人旅客可以免费携带身高不到1.2m的儿童一名。

- The fare of child's ticket is fifty percent of the adult ticket, the fare of berth ticket is the same as the adult ticket.

  儿童票票价按成人票价的50%计算，卧铺票与成人相同。

- The child's destination should not exceed that of the accompanying adult.

  与成年旅客通行的儿童，到站不能超过成人的到站。

- The child who is taller than 1.5 meters is required to buy an adult ticket.

  身高超过1.5m的儿童，乘火车应买成人票。

- If more than one, the other should buy a child's ticket.

  超过一名儿童时，超过的人数应买儿童票。

- The child from 1.2 meters to 1.5 meters in height are required to buy a child's ticket of the same kind of seat as the accompanying adult when taking the train.

  身高1.2~1.5m的小孩乘车时，应随同成人购买座别相同的儿童客票。

- Your child is already over 1.1 meters, please buy a children ticket.

  您的孩子已超过1.1m了，请买儿童票。

- Your child is already over 1.4 meters, please buy an adult ticket.

  您的孩子已超过1.4m了，请买成人票。

- You have taken two children. One is over 1.2 meters, the other is less than 1.2 meters in height. You are required to buy a berth ticket and two child's tickets for them.

  您带了两个孩子，一个身高超过1.2m，另一个未超过1.2m。您要买一张卧铺票和两张儿童客票。

- Two children may share one berth.

  两名儿童可以共用一个卧铺。

- You have got together with your two children under 1.2 meters in height. You are required to buy a berth ticket and a child's ticket.

  您带了两名不到1.2m的儿童，需要买一张卧铺票和一张儿童客票。

2.Security Check Service Expressions

- Security check, please!

  请安检！

- This way, please.

  请这边走。

- Follow me, please.

  请跟我走。

- Please show me your ID card.

  请出示您的身份证。

- Ok, please go in/ahead.

  好了，请往里面走。

- Sorry, your passport is a bit of problem. Please wait a moment.

  不好意思，您的证件有点问题，请稍等一下。

- Please wait behind the yellow line.

  请在黄线外稍等。

- Please be patient.

 请耐心等候。
- Sorry, this is for staff only.

 对不起，这是员工通道。
- Please put your baggage on the conveyor belt of the machine please.

 请把你的行李放在传送带上。
- Please pass through the detector one by one.

 请一个一个通过探测门。
- Please put all your metallic objects such as coin, cellphone, chewing gum, cigarettes, and anything with aluminum foil into the basket.

 请把您随身携带的所有金属物品，如硬币、手机、口香糖、香烟以及带锡纸的物品等放在篮子里。
- Could you hold the baby in your arms and let the pram be checked by the X-ray machine?

 您可以抱起婴儿，将婴儿车通过X光机检查吗？
- Excuse me, sir. Please take your computer out and put it in the basket.

 对不起，先生，请把您的电脑从包里取出放入筐里。
- Anything else in your pocket?

 口袋里还有其他物品吗？
- I'm sorry to tell you that flammable items cannot be taken with you into the train.

 很抱歉告诉您，易燃品不能随身带上火车。
- Please come over for inspection.

 请过来接受检查。
- Please raise your arms.

 请您抬起双臂。
- Turn around, please.

 请转身。
- Please unbutton your coat.

 请把您的衣扣打开。
- I'm sorry to tell you that it is a prohibited item. You can't take it with you into the aircraft.

 很抱歉告诉您，这是违禁品，您不能把它带上飞机。
- Checking is done, thank you for your corporation.

 检查完毕，感谢您的配合。
- You can take your luggage now.

 您可以拿行李了。
- These items are forbidden by law and will have to be confiscated.

 这些东西是违禁品，我们必须没收。
- We could check it in for you, or you could have it deposited temporarily at our place for up to one month.

 您可以办理托运或在我们这儿办理一个月内的暂存。
- This is the government's rule. For your own safety and other passengers, we need your understanding and corporation.

 这是政府规定的，为了您和其他旅客的安全，请您理解和配合我们的工作。

- Please take away your luggage and wish you have a pleasant journey.
请带好您的行李，祝您旅途愉快。
- No Dangerous goods are allowed to bring on the train!
严禁携带危险品上车！
- These are inflammables, please leave them to our care.
这些是易燃品，请交给我们适当处理。

3. Waiting Service Expressions

- No smoking here please.
请勿抽烟。
- Please Keep the Reading Matter in the Business Class Lounge.
请勿将读物带出商务候车室。
- Ticket, please. Have your ticket back.
您的票！请把票拿好。
- Your passport, please.
请出示您的护照。
- Excuse me, please show your ticket on demand.
您好，请出示您的车票。
- Hello, please unfold your ticket, thank you.
您好！请打开您的车票，谢谢。
- Sorry, your luggage is overweight, please buy a luggage ticket.
对不起，您的行李已超重，请补票。
- Please add more...yuan for your ticket.
您需要加补……元钱。
- You are welcome. Please wait at the platform. Your ticket will be checked first, then you can board the train.
不用客气。请您在站台等候，先检票再上车。
- Passengers could come into the waiting room six hours before the departing time.
旅客可在开车前6小时进入候车室候车。
- Please get your tickets and luggage ready.
请把车票准备好，拿好行李。
- Passengers for G51 please go to the boarding gate for ticket checking.
乘坐G51次的旅客请到检票口检票。
- It's boarding time for train T2, please.
现在请乘坐T2次的旅客请登车。
- Get into the station one by one please.
请按顺序进站。
- Ticket and ID Check Ends 20 Minutes before Departure.
开车前20分钟停止验证。
- Ticket Gates Will Close 3 Minutes before Departure.
开车前3分钟停止检票。

4. Carriage Service Expressions

- Mind your steps.

注意脚下。
- The other end of the coach.

在车厢的那一端。
- Just wait a moment. Ok?

稍等会，好吗？
- Sorry, I don't quite understand you. Please speak slowly.

抱歉，我没听懂，您说慢一点。
- Welcome aboard our train. I'll be at your service during the whole journey.

欢迎乘坐我们的列车，我将全程为您服务。
- Please keep gateways clear.

请保持过道畅通。
- Please take your belongings with you.

请带好自己的行李物品。
- We are looking forward to having you here again.

我们期待着您下次乘车。
- The destination will be reached in about twenty minutes.

还有大约20分钟到达终点站。
- Our train currently travels at 90 kilometers per hour.

现在的速度大概90km/h。
- The toilets are available only when the train is traveling.

停车厕所是要锁闭的，请开车后再使用。
- The train pulling in, toilet is unavailable now, please wait several minutes.

马上要到站了，现在不能使用厕所，请稍等几分钟。
- Please show me your ticket, it says which seat is yours.

给我看一下您的车票，上面有您的座位号。
- Excuse me, I need to get a pass. Can I help you with your bags? Can I move it please?

打扰一下，借过。我能帮您提包吗？我能移开它吗？
- Please take care of your valuables.

请保管好您的贵重物品！
- Help us to keep the train clean.

请协助我们，保持火车清洁卫生。
- Take care when you get off the train.

下车时当心。
- Luggage must not be put in the gateway.

行李不允许放到过道上。
- Mind the gap.

请小心台阶间跨度。
- The train is now ... minutes late.

列车现在晚点……分钟。
- Please don't worry, the train will arrive on schedule.

请别着急，列车将正点到达。
- The train will soon be on schedule.

列车很快就会正点的。

- This is a temporary stop.

现在是临时停车。

- It stays for ... minutes.

停车……分。

- Please don't get off the train.

请不要下车。

5.Dinging Service Expression

- Our restaurant opens at 6:00 pm for supper.

餐车下午6点开始供应晚餐。

- Good evening. Welcome to our dining car.

晚上好，欢迎就餐。

- For how many?

您几位？

- This way, please.

您这边请。

- Here is the menu.

给您菜单。

- What would you like to have?

您想吃点什么？

- Anything to drink?

您喝点什么？

- Welcome to the dining car.

欢迎您到餐车用餐。

- Do you mind sitting by the window?

您靠窗户坐好吗？

- Are you having lunch?

您要吃午饭吗？

- What would you like for dinner?

您晚餐想吃点什么？

- What kind of dishes will you have?

您想点什么菜？

- What would you like to drink?

您喜欢喝点什么？

- Which kind of drinks do you prefer?

您想点什么饮料？

- May I recommend Qingdao beer? It's very famous.

我推荐青岛啤酒可以吗？非常有名的。

- After the train set off, the crew members of the dining car will serve food with trolley carts. Please wait patiently. The trolley carts serve snacks, soft drink, beer and boxed meals. You can also shop in Carriage 5.

开车后餐车工作人员将流动售货，请您耐心等候。餐车出售小食品、饮料、酒水、盒饭等，您也可到5号车厢选购。

- Sorry, we don't accept foreign currency. We accept Chinese RMB, Alipay and

WeChat.

对不起，我们不收外币。您可以使用人民币、支付宝和微信付款。

• Good morning/afternoon, Sir! Let me unfold the tray table for you. This is your milk and coffee. Enjoy your food.

先生您好，我帮您把托盘桌打开，这是您的牛奶和咖啡，请您慢用。

• If you need any food, please let me know. l will ask the attendants of the dining car to order it for and bring it over.

如果您需要用餐，请告诉我，我会及时通知餐车人员为您点餐并送餐。

• Good morning/afternoon, Sir! Let me open the small table for you. The tea and coffee are prepared for you. Please enjoy yourself.

先生您好，我帮您把小桌打开，这是列车为您准备的茶水和咖啡，请您慢用。

• If you need any food, please let me know. l will ask the attendants of the dining car to send the food to you.

如果您需要用餐，请告诉我，我会及时通知餐车人员为您点餐并送餐。

6.Special and Emergency Service Expressions

• What's the matter?

您有什么不舒服？

• I'll call a ambulance for you at once.

我马上联系救护车。

• If it is inconvenient for you, I can arrange a nearby seat for you.

您行动不便，就近乘坐吧，我来帮您安排。

• Sir, please make sure this baby cartridge won't move.

先生，您携带的婴儿车一定要踩好脚闸。

• This is a toilet for the disabled, equipped with a handrail and Emergency Call Button.

这里是残疾人卫生间，里面设有扶手、紧急呼叫按钮。

• Mind you steps and walk slowly. The platform is slippery. Let me help you with the luggage.

站台较滑，您下车时要注意，您慢一点，我来帮您拿行李。

• You'd better consult a doctor soon/go to see a doctor soon.

您最好早点去看医生。

• Hope you'll recover soon.

祝您早日康复。

• Hello, the train is running very fast. Please take good care of your child and be careful.

您好，列车车速较快，请您看管好小朋友，注意安全。

• Dear passengers, I am cleaning up the compartment for you. The train is arriving very soon. Please take care of your luggage in case you might take the wrong luggage or leave it behind on the train.

各位旅客：我为您清理一下包房卫生，快到站了，请您收拾好您的物品，防止拿错或遗忘行李。

• When you get off the train, be sure to with you your luggage, especially the valuables, such as the wallet and the passport. Don't leave them behind on the train.

下车时请带好您的随身物品，特别是贵重物品，如钱包、护照等，不要遗忘在列车上。

• Thank you very much for your valuable/precious suggestions. Your suggestions are very helpful to our work. I hope you will enjoy a better service from us when you take the train next time.

非常感谢您为我们工作提出宝贵意见，您的意见对我们的工作有很大的帮助，希望在您下次乘坐我们列车时，能看到我们更好的工作表现。

• Sir, thank you for your valuable suggestions. We will report to our supervisor. We hope you will frequently take our train and help us improve our service. Thanks.

先生：非常感谢您给我们提出的宝贵意见，我会向我们的上级反馈。希望您能经常乘坐我们列车，帮助我们完善工作中的不足，谢谢！

• In case of emergency evacuation, use hammer to break the emergency escape window to escape from the car when the train has come to stop. Hold the handle of the hammer and pull it out with strength when the seal breaks automatically. Hit the window hard on the mark and use the handle to push the glass remains outside the train, paying attention to your hand.

遇突发紧急情况需要迅速组织逃生疏散时，在列车停稳的情况下，可使用破窗锤击打车厢紧急逃生窗逃生。握住紧急破窗锤把手，用力向外侧拔出，拔出时铅封即开，对准车窗上击打位置标记用力击打，利用把手外侧将未完全脱落的玻璃推向车体外侧，注意操作时手的安全。

• SOS buttons are equipped in on-board restrooms (including those for the disabled).

车内卫生间(包括无障碍卫生间)设有SOS按钮。

• Press SOS buttons for assistance in case of emergencies in restrooms.

当您在卫生间内发生突发情况需要帮助时，可按下SOS按钮。

• Please do not fill your cup too full with hot water, especially when using paper or plastic cups, and keep children from fetching hot water alone in case they get scalded.

您在接开水时，不要过满，使用纸杯和塑料杯的旅客要特别小心。请勿让儿童独自倒开水，以免烫伤。

• Please do not push or lean against the door or put the hand on the door edge or the junction between the carriages in case any injury occurs.

乘坐列车时，请勿挤、靠车门，请不要把手扶在门缝处或车厢连接处以防挤伤。

• When adjusting the seat, please pay attention to the articles, such as a cup or a laptop, placed on the tray table attached to your seatback, in case the passenger behind you gets scalded or the articles get damaged.

小桌板与前排座椅相连，前排乘客调整座椅时，请您留意后排小桌板旅客放置的水杯、电脑等物品，以免造成烫伤或物品损坏。

• Please do not use fire extinguishers, fire alarm buttons, emergency braking lever or any other safety equipment without good reason; please do not get near to or enter into the driver's cab without authorization.

请勿随意扳动(按下)灭火器、火灾报警按钮、紧急制动按钮、紧急制动手柄等安全设备。

• Please do not linger around or enter into the driver's-cab without permission.

不得擅自靠近或闯入司机室。

• In case of train delay, temporary power failure, air-conditioning breakdown, fire, explosion or other emergencies, please keep calm, follow the instructions of the train staff, maintain good order and leave your belongings behind for later retrieval.

动车组列车运行途中遇列车晚点、临时停电、空调故障、火灾、爆炸等紧急情况，请您不要惊慌，听从列车工作人员的指挥，保持良好的秩序，不要急于拿物品。

• Train staff shall launch emergency plans immediately and carry out emergency response in accordance with the procedure rules.

列车全体工作人员将立即启动应急预案，按规定程序做好应急处置。

• Please leave us your contact number .We'll inform you as soon as we have any news.

请留下您的联系方式，有消息我马上通知您。

• Dear passengers, it's a temporary stop. The train can't move on for the signal system problem. We are very sorry for any inconvenience.

旅客朋友们，现在是临时停车。由于前方无运行信号，列车不能继续运行。因此给您带来的不便，请您见谅。

• We are very sorry that we do not know the reason for the delay. We'll-inform you if there is any news. We are very sorry.

对不起，晚点原因现在还不清楚，有消息我会通知大家，请原谅！

References

[1] 张晓鹏, 李茜, 刘卓瑛, 等. 高速铁路客运乘务专业英语课程融入式教学模式研究[J]. 张家口职业技术学院学报, 2020.

[2] 陆志慧, 田丰. "一带一路"倡议背景下江苏城市公示语英译现状调查分析[J]. 产业与科技论坛, 2020.

[3] 李俊娴, 梁烨. 基于"智慧职教"平台的《高铁乘务英语》混合式教学实践研究[J]. 校园英语, 2020.

[4] 李金书. 高速铁路服务英语教学现状及对策探析[J]. 佳木斯职业学院学报, 2019.

[5] 肖璧莹. "互联网+"时代下铁路类高职专业英语研究[J]. 校园英语, 2019.

[6] 潘自影. 铁路客运英语[M]. 成都:西南交通大学出版社, 2018.

[7] 韩志花. "乌大张"合作区高校高铁乘务专业英语教学的现状及对策[J]. 学园, 2018.

[8] 王蕊. 高职《铁路客运服务英语》课程教学体系探究[J]. 中国校外教育(美术), 2014.

[9] 伍帅英, 应婷婷. 轨道交通专业英语[M]. 北京:中国铁道出版社, 2014.

[10] 吴宝明. 轨道交通行业英语[M]. 北京:外语教学与研究出版社, 2013.

[11] 惠利霞, 高琦. 铁路客运业务实用英语[M]. 北京:中国铁道出版社, 2013.

[12] 魏宏, 周际. 铁路客运英语综合教程[M]. 北京:中国铁道出版社, 2013.

[13] 惠利霞, 高琦. 铁路客运业务实用英语[M]. 北京:中国铁道出版社, 2013.

[14] 梁伟. 高速铁路实用英语口语[M]. 北京:中国铁道出版社, 2012.

[15] 北京铁路局. 高铁车站客运实用英语[M]. 北京:中国铁道出版社, 2011.

[16] 魏宏. 铁路客服英语辨析与规范[J]. 黑河学刊, 2011.

[17] 《铁路客运英语工作手册》编委会. 铁路客运英语工作手册[M]. 北京:中国铁道出版社, 2011.

[18] 北京铁路局. 高铁车站客运实用英语[M]. 北京:中国铁道出版社, 2011.

[19] 倪华. 高速铁路服务英语[M]. 成都:西南交通大学出版社, 2010.